Francisco José de Caldas

A Scientist at Work in Nueva Granada

TRANSACTIONS

of the

American Philosophical Society

Held at Philadelphia for Promoting Useful Knowledge

VOLUME 84, Part 5, 1994

Francisco José de Caldas
A Scientist at Work in Nueva Granada

JOHN WILTON APPEL

THE AMERICAN PHILOSOPHICAL SOCIETY

Independence Square, Philadelphia

1994

Library of Congress Catalog
Card Number: 94-71521
International Standard Book Number 0-87169-845-5
US ISSN 0065-9746

TABLE OF CONTENTS

ILLUSTRATIONS

A SCIENTIST IN SEARCH OF COMMUNITY
1796–1802

Francisco José de Caldas y Tenorio was born[1] in 1768 in Popayán, a provincial capital in the Spanish colony Nuevo Reino de Granada. The eighteenth century had brought the beginnings of institutionalized science to this part of America. In the first half of the century France sent an expedition to the equator to learn the true figure of the Earth. In the latter half the Spanish crown's interest in the natural resources of its colonies led to the formation of the Botanical Expedition. The Expedition's director—José Celestino Mutis—dedicated his life to the study of the flora and fauna of the region and in the process built the foundations of an active scientific community.

However, the health of the scientific enterprise should not be overstated. Spain maintained strict control not only over the colonies' access to books but also other Europeans' access to the colonies. The Church's influence still affected in an adverse way the assimilation of new ideas, such as Copernicanism.

Caldas, with a fervent interest in science and lacking the educational resources and personal contacts available in Europe, developed a scientific program based on what was available to him. He became an avid observer of the geography of his surroundings while learning to make astronomical measurements of latitude and longitude, and barometric measurements of altitude. Caldas kept travel diaries and made maps, and he began to take an interest in botany, at the same time maintaining an active correspondence regarding his work with a small number of friends.

In 1801 Caldas independently discovered the hypsometric principle and fabricated his own hypsometric thermometer. This illustrated, however, his lack of contact with organized science, because he had no way of knowing the originality of his discovery. The arrival of the Prussian naturalist, Alexander von Humboldt, brought to a head Caldas's discontent with his own isolation from the European community. Although events did not converge as Caldas had hoped, he enjoyed the most intense period of scientific activity in his life.

---

[1] Caldas's baptismal certificate has been published in the periodical *Revista Popayán*, No. 261, Ano XXV, 24 March 1957, p. 41; and reprinted in the newspaper *El Liberal*, Popayán, 18 November 1986, p. 6.

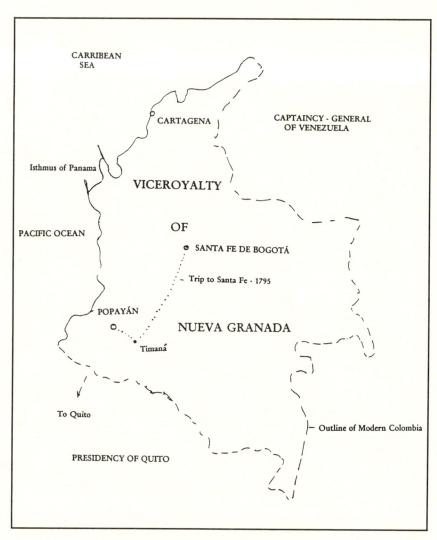

MAP 1.
A Scientist in Search of Community, 1796–1802.

I. CHOOSING THE SCIENTIST'S PATH

Caldas in Brief

Caldas was the fifth of fifteen children born to José de Caldas, a Spaniard by birth, and Vicenta Tenorio, who belonged to a well established Creole family. The family was of modest circumstances, landowners, but by no means wealthy.

The details of Caldas's early years are sketchy. We know, however, that he attended the Seminario Mayor de Popayán for his secondary school education. At the time this was one of three schools in the viceroyalty of Nueva Granada that offered instruction in mathematics and the sciences. The others were located in the capital of the viceroyalty, Santa Fe de Bogotá. In the capital José Celestino Mutis, director of the Botanical Expedition, had initiated the first professorship of mathematics in the colony in the Colegio Mayor de Nuestra Señora del Rosario. Later on, a similar professorship was established in the Colegio de San Bartólome. Caldas's professor at the Seminario Mayor was Felix Restrepo, a native of the province of Antioquia, who had taken private lessons from Mutis in Bogotá. Caldas praised Restrepo as:

. . . an enlightened teacher, who detested that scholastic jargon. . . . Under his guidance I applied myself to the study of arithmetic, geometry, trigonometry, algebra and experimental physics, because our philosophy course was really a course of physics and mathematics.[1]

That Caldas had the opportunity to study mathematics at all was a departure from the past. Yet though he was captivated by the sciences his father insisted that he study law after he finished his course work at the Seminario. Caldas accepted with resignation. In 1783 he began his studies at the Colegio Mayor del Rosario in Bogotá. He earned his degree in 1793 and returned immediately to Popayán.

Caldas's letters show him to have had a mercurial temperament. There are examples of innocence and worldliness, piety and cynicism, generosity and selfishness, love and hate. He was, however, constant in his interest in furthering the cause of science and in improving the situation of his native land. As for his physical appearance, the following description is given by his first biographer, Lino de Pombo:

Caldas was of normal stature and robust complexion; tan, rounded face, wide forehead, the dark eyes somewhat melancholic, hair black and straight, short

---

[1] Jorge Arias de Greiff, et al., ed. *Cartas de Caldas*. Academia Colombiana de Ciencias Exactas, Fisicas y Naturales. Bogotá. 1978, p. 99.

FIGURE 1.   Portrait of Caldas. From *Obras Completas de Francisco José de Caldas*. Universidad Nacional de Colombia. Imprenta Nacional. Bogotá. 1966.

neck, his stride easy but slow and contemplative. He ordinarily wore a frock coat of dark cloth which he buttoned and unbuttoned continually, changing the lapel with the result that the buttons did not last long; and he was never found without a small flexible cane in the hand nor a piece of fine twisted tobacco in his mouth. He was clean but not tidy in his dress, with soft manners, a friendly disposition and agreeable conversation.[2]

Before entering into a discussion of Caldas's development as a scientist in the period 1796–1802, two factors that were of fundamental importance to him should be introduced—the French expedition to measure the shape of the earth and the Botanical Expedition of Nueva Granada.

THE SHAPE OF THE EARTH

In 1735 the Paris Academy of Sciences took upon itself the task of determining the shape of the earth. According to Newton the earth varied from a perfect sphere by a thickening or oblateness at the equator. The astronomer Cassini held the opposite view—that the earth was prolate or fatter near the poles. The response of the Academy to this controversy was the formation of two expeditions to measure directly the length of one degree of longitudinal arc, near the north pole and near the equator. The polar expedition, led by Maupertius, was sent to Lapland. The equatorial expedition was directed to the presidency of Quito in Spanish America.

The members of the equatorial expedition were Louis Godin, Charles Marie de la Condamine and Pierre Bouger. They were joined by the naturalist Joseph de Jussieu and two Spanish naval officers, Antonio de Ulloa and Jorge Juan y Santacilla, who had been sent by the Spanish government to oversee the operations of the expedition. They landed in the port city of Monta on 10 March 1736 and arrived at Quito in June. The measurements of the longitudinal arc were made on the Yaruqui plain. These consisted of both topographic measurements of length and astronomical determination of the latitude of the endpoints of the arc. (The work of the expedition was marked by internal discord resulting in separate observations being made by Godin, Bouger and La Condamine, and by Juan and Ulloa.) When their work was done the "academiciens" left pyramids at the endpoints and a marble plaque inscribed with their results at a Jesuit church in Quito.

The coming of the French expedition to Quito was a cultural as well as a scientific event. It had the effect of pointing out the geographic peculiarity of the region—in this case the position of the earth's equator. Similarly, earlier observations of the tropical flora and later interest in the great volcanos of the region were convincing evidence for the inhabitants of the Spanish colonies that there was something special about the nat-

---

[2] Lino de Pombo. "Francisco José de Caldas, Biografía del Sabio." *Suplemento de la Revista de la Academia Colombiana de Ciencias Exactas, Físicas y Naturales.* Libreria Voluntad. Bogotá. 1958, p. 47.

ural world which surrounded them – special enough to invite the attention of European scientists.

Caldas was an avid student of the work of the expedition which he referred to as "la expedición de La Condamine." He profited from the multiplicity of written works produced by the various members. He had read Bouger's *La Figure de la Terre* and La Condamine's *Mens des trois degres* and *Introduccion Historique*. From Bouger's *La Figure de la Terre* Caldas learned how to calculate altitudes from barometer readings. From the *Observaciones Astronómicas* of Jorge Juan he learned to determine positions by astronomical measurements. It also served as a guide to Caldas's construction of his own instruments. There are also references in Caldas's letters to the works of La Condamine.

Of further importance to Caldas's scientific work is the visit made by La Condamine in February 1737 to the province of Loja, south of Quito, on his way to Lima to solve the financial difficulties of the expedition. Loja was well-known for the production of cinchona bark (see Chapter VI), used for making the anti-malarial drug, quinine. However, there had been no careful observation of the cinchona tree by European naturalists. La Condamine made careful drawings of the plant and later sent them to the Swedish botanist Linnaeus. The drawings were the basis of Linnaeus's classification of the tree as "cinchona officinalis" (now called "cinchona lancifolia").

The work of the "academiciens" was a fundamental reference point for Caldas. During his stay in Quito between 1802 and 1805 he made every effort to retrace their paths (see Chapter V). In addition, Mutis's interest in the cinchona tree led him to support Caldas's trip to Loja in 1804.

THE BOTANICAL EXPEDITION

We must, at this point, introduce a second institution that was fundamental to Caldas's career.

The Spanish "conquistadores" came to America hoping to return to the Iberian peninsula laden with the fabled treasures of the great Indian civilizations. Yet, although they sought the gold of "El Dorado," their most important discoveries were the new and useful plant specimens they found. Among the most important of these were maize, potatoes, tobacco, cacao and cinchona bark. Early travelers, especially the Jesuit priests, brought home travel diaries describing the rich and varied flora of the New World. They described the uses of different crops, herbal medicines and dyes.

In the latter half of the eighteenth century the Spanish crown became seriously interested in the study of the natural resources of its colonies. Expeditions were established in the Philippines, the Viceroyalty of Peru, Nueva España (Mexico) and the Viceroyalty of Nueva Granada. The Botanical Expedition in Nueva Granada was the result of the initiative of José Celestino Mutis who, though a physician by training, had since his arrival in 1760 become a dedicated observer of the natural world in

the Andes. Mutis found an enthusiastic patron in the viceroy (and archbishop) Caballero y Gongora. The viceroy suggested to the king of Spain
the formation of the expedition in 1782, and the official decree was signed
on 1 November 1783. (It is significant to note that the other expeditions
were established by royal initiative, whereas Mutis petitioned the crown
for the expedition to Nueva Granada, from the outset a highly personal
effort.)

The expedition was to be created ". . . upon the example of the Botanical Expedition . . . undertaken in equatorial America"[3]—that is, the
expedition to the Viceroyalty of Peru. According to the decree the scope
of activities was:

> . . . the methodical examination of the natural products of my dominions in
> America, not only to promote progress in the physical sciences but also to banish
> the doubts and quarrels that are found in medicine, dyes and other important
> arts, and to augment commerce, and that there be formed herbaria and collec-
> tions of natural products, describing and delineating the plants found in those
> fertile provinces of mine to enrich my collection of natural history and botanical
> garden of the court, and sending to Spain seed and live roots of the most useful
> plants and trees, signaling those that are used, or should be used as medicine
> and for naval construction, so that they be acclimated in the appropriate climates
> of this peninsula, without omitting the astronomical and geographical observa-
> tions that can be made along with the advances in these sciences. . . .[4]

In establishing the first scientific institution in Nueva Granada, King
Carlos III named Mutis "my first botanist and astronomer" and provided
him with an annual salary of $2,000 pesos, in addition to a special grant
of $2,000 pesos so that Mutis could complete work he had undertaken
prior to the formation of the expedition. Furthermore, the expedition
was to receive an unspecified number of books and instruments from
Spain. It is worth noting here that although Spain was criticized (and
especially so by Caldas) for closing off communication between Europe
and the Spanish colonies, thus leaving the region scientifically back-
ward, in the case of the creation of the Botanical Expedition the crown
was generous in its financial and moral support. This can be attributed
in part to the enthusiasm of Mutis, who was born in Spain, and his good
relations with Viceroy Caballero y Gongora.

The expedition, after a sixty-day stay in the region of Mesa de Juan
Diaz, established its first headquarters in the town of Mariquita, located
along the Magdalena River. Joining Mutis was his second-in-command,
Eloy Valenzuela, a priest like Mutis (Mutis had been ordained in 1772)
and Pablo Antonio Garcia, the first of a succession of painters who
worked for the expedition. During the eight years that followed work
was done on a variety of topics. Members of the expedition exposed them-

---

[3] A. Federico Gredilla. *Biografia de José Celestino Mutis y sus Observaciones sobre las Vigilias
y Sueños de Algunas Plantas*. Academia Colombiana de Historia. Plaza and Janes. Bogotá.
1982, p. 146.
[4] Ibid., 146.

selves to snakebites in order to test venom antidotes made from herbs. Mutis organized the production and commerce of cinchona bark. The viceroy sponsored the visit of the Mexican José D'Elhuyar to aid Mutis in the evaluation of mineral deposits.

In 1790 a new viceroy, José de Ezpletia, called the expedition back to Santa Fe de Bogotá. Valenzuela had retired and was replaced by Francisco Antonio Zea, a native of the province of Antioquia. A new director of painters, Salvador Rizo, was named and a school for painters was established. The training of competent illustrators was a constant concern for Mutis since drawings of the plants that had been collected were vital for the documentation of the work of the expedition. Students were solicited and there was no tuition. Many of the painters who worked for the expedition came from the presidency of Quito, although both Rizo and Francisco Javier Matis were Granadian artists.

Soon the Botanical Expedition's importance became more than being the sole scientific enterprise in viceroyalty. It had become a cultural institution as well. By 1794 the staff included Mutis, Zea, Rizo, a secretary, 13 painters (on full-time and contractual bases), a custodian of collections, several correspondents and members ad honorem, including Mutis's nephews, José de Mutis and Sinforoso Mutis.

The presence of the expedition and the spirit of free scientific inquiry mixed well with the pro-independence sentiments already felt in the colonial capital. Indeed, in 1795 members of the expedition were imprisoned for the translation of censored materials and the distribution of anti-royalist literature (see Chapter X).

Although the Botanical Expedition was a creation of Spain, it soon became part of the fabric of life in Nueva Granada. Mutis was successful in establishing strong foundations and building upon them. His persistence and enthusiasm (and certainly also his longevity) gave Bogotá the continual presence of a scientific enterprise whose liberating effects surpassed the intellectual realm and spread into the political world as well.

A Self-Taught Scientist

After his graduation from law school in 1793, Caldas returned to Popayán and settled into the normal rhythm of life in the provincial capital. His position teaching civil law and perhaps a private practice of the affairs of his family's landholdings left him little time for other concerns. The interest he had taken in the sciences as a student at the Seminario was effectively abandoned. But sometime in 1794 or 1795 he fell ill with an unspecified disease. Weakened and unable to maintain his concentration, he was not only forced to give up his teaching position but his doctors prohibited reading and all other forms of mental exertion as well.

Faced with this obligatory inactivity Caldas took the unlikely decision of becoming an itinerant merchant. He crossed the central mountain range ("cordillera central") which lies to the east of Popayán and carried his wares to the towns and villages (Neiva, Timaná, Pital, Gigante) in the tropical zone at the eastern base of the cordillera. Here Caldas found himself free of the demands of his profession and the obligations of society in Popayán. It was this break with his daily routine that brought Caldas a fresh interest in the natural world.

Thus in 1796 Caldas decided to dedicate himself to science. He left temporarily his work as a merchant (though his resources were limited he apparently had other means of supporting himself) to travel to the colonial capital, Santa Fe de Bogotá. Caldas, well aware of his lack of training, went to Bogotá to find books and instruments that were not available to him in Popayán. It was probably this trip to Bogotá that brought him into contact with the works published by the members of the French expedition of 1735. He may also have become acquainted with some of the works of Buffon and Linnaeus. In his letters Caldas mentions having read in Bogotá a book on astronomy by Lalande and navigational tables by Besout which he copied. In addition he purchased ". . . a compass, a marine barometer, two thermometers and a reflecting octant."[5]

Caldas was anxious to put his instruments to use. In August 1796 he carried his barometer to measure the height of the Guadalupe peak which overlooks Bogotá. By October, when he began his return trip to Popayán, Caldas had a program to follow. He kept a travel diary of his trip. (This diary and many other of Caldas's manuscripts are lost.) Along the way Caldas measured altitudes with his barometer, air temperature with his thermometers, latitudes with a gnomon he had made and noted his observations on those things that interested him, particularly geographical and meteorological observations.

As he continued on his journey, Caldas passed through the village of Timaná where he was informed of a dispute regarding the municipal boundaries. It is not clear whether Caldas offered his services or was sought out by the inhabitants, but in any case he jumped at the opportunity and took up the problem of making a map of Timaná. He worked from December 1797 to February 1798 making use of a lunar eclipse on 3 December 1797 to establish the longitude of Timaná. Astronomical determinations of longitude were a favorite activity of Caldas. In the course of his trips in Nueva Granada and in the presidency of Quito he used lunar eclipses, stellar occultations and occultations of the Galilean satellites to determine the longitudes of the towns and villages through which he passed. To his dismay, the inhabitants of Timaná later replaced Caldas's map with another. "I am saddened that the work of three months, of a terrible number of astronomical, geodesic . . . observations have been left in darkness and without use. . . ."[6]

The limitations of being a scientist without community became clear to Caldas through his main activity of this period—astronomy. Here,

---

[5] Eduardo Posada, ed. *Cartas de Caldas*. Biblioteca de Historia Nacional. Volume 15. Imprenta Nacional. 1917, p. 86. Caldas's most frequent correspondents were his friends Santiago Arroyo and Antonio Arboleda, and his mentor José Celestino Mutis.

[6] Ibid., 34.

Caldas began from scratch. He started by building a gnomon with which he came to know the movements of the Sun and to measure latitude. Using Jorge Juan's *Observaciones Astronómicas* as a guide, he directed craftsmen in Popayán in the construction of a quadrant. He took a pendulum from an old clock to make a chronometer and learned to determine longitudes by the observation of astronomical events and comparison with ephemerides. In the patio of his parent's home he raised a platform which constituted his observatory.

This solitary enthusiasm is certainly noteworthy since in the late 1700s Popayán, with a population of perhaps 10,000, offered the nascent astronomer no material or spiritual support. Caldas knew that his work was only a beginning and fretted about the lack of interaction with other astronomers. He wrote of his problems to his friend, Santiago Arroyo, "I lose heart when I see so little astronomy in all of Nueva Granada and there is not one person to be asked to measure a latitude."[7]

Furthermore, Caldas himself was unaware of some of the bare essentials:

Now you know that astronomers signal the stars using Greek characters. . . . I have seen them but I do not know their names to be able to enunciate them. I hope that you will send me a Greek alphabet, well written, giving each letter with its name and the corresponding letter in our alphabet.[8]

He was also unable to obtain them, "How it distresses me to see Jupiter, surrounded by its moons, sail above my head, prepare all that is necessary and not be able to observe one single eclipse for the lack of astronomical tables!"[9]

But Caldas persevered. He found an ephemerides from the Spanish observatory in Cadiz and asked his friend Santiago Arroyo to find astronomical tables and the second volume of Lalande's treatise on astronomy. He found, in Popayán, some lenses and built his own refracting telescope which apparently served him well, ". . . I can see perfectly the ring of Saturn, the satellites of Jupiter and the dark zones of this planet."[10]

Later, he learned that there was a larger achromatic telescope in Cali and arranged for its purchase. His pursuit of astronomy brought Caldas the satisfaction he had sought in the study of nature. He describes his first session with his home-made refractor, "It was one o'clock in the morning and I could leave neither the sky nor my telescope. Saturn and Jupiter came and went in my imagination; the zones, the ring, the satellites, all of this filled my soul with pleasure and contentment."[11]

Although Caldas had no contact with other scientists during this period, not even with the members of the Botanical Expedition, he was fully aware of the need for communication in the scientific enterprise.

---

[7] Ibid., 22.
[8] Ibid., 20.
[9] Ibid., 24.
[10] Ibid., 23.
[11] Ibid., 26.

Thus, faced with a lack of community, he made his own. Caldas's enthusiasm was persistent and contagious. He pestered his friend Arroyo in Bogotá for books, maps and ephemerides. He convinced Arroyo to borrow a telescope to function as a co-observer, and when Caldas announced, "For nearly two years I have kept a diary of all the variations of our atmosphere; thunder rain and drought. . . ."[12] it is part of an effort to enlist Arroyo as a meteorological observer as well. In Popayán Caldas organized a small group of friends, including Antonio Arboleda who was a frequent correspondent, into a scientific circle. They often went on field trips to the surrounding countryside taking along mules and Indian servants to carry Caldas's instruments. In addition, Caldas found in Popayán his first patron, Manuel Maria Arboleda, whom Caldas called ". . . my friend and protector. . . ."[13] Manuel Arboleda purchased books chosen by Caldas including works of Linnaeus, and it was Manuel Arboleda who purchased the achromatic telescope found in Cali. Thus, although Caldas was far from the mainstream of the scientific world, he knew which direction to take.

Besides communication with colleagues and the search for patronage another fundamental of the scientific enterprise is the publication of results. When Caldas read in *Correo Curioso*, a new periodical inaugurated in Bogotá, an incorrect estimate of the height of the Guadalupe and Monserrate peaks, he decided to act. In May 1801 he put to paper the barometric measurements he had made of Guadalupe in August 1796 together with his subsequent calculations of altitude.

Caldas's debt to the French "academiciens" became clear as his work progressed. For the calculation of altitudes from barometric readings Caldas presented different methods. One was that given by Bouger in *Voyage au Perou*. To check the result Caldas used a method given by Jorge Juan in *Observaciones Astronómicas* based on an arithmetic progression and using the Caraburu peak near Quito as a baseline.

Caldas published his article in the July and August 1801 issues of *Correo Curioso* concluding that Guadalupe lies some 1,682 toises above sea level.[14] With this publication Caldas took his first step toward becoming part of the scientific community in Nueva Granada.

---

[12] Ibid., 41.

[13] Ibid., 31.: Manuel Maria Arboleda (1767–1818) was a brother of Caldas's friend, Antonio Arboleda (see Appendix C). He was a priest and professor of law. He purchased several books on science for Caldas.

[14] Caldas used the following units:

toises (toesas): 1 toise = 1.81 meters
inches (pulgadas): Bateman* argues that Caldas used neither the English inch (1 inch = 25.4 mm) nor the old Spanish inch (1 inch = 23.22 mm); rather, Caldas's own data correspond to a value of 1 inch = 27.14 mm. The inch was subdivided into 12 lines.

* Alfredo D. Bateman. *Francisco José de Caldas: El Hombre y El Sabio*. Departamento de Caldas. Colombia. 1954, p. 139.

II. CALDAS DISCOVERS THE HYPSOMETRIC PRINCIPLE

The year 1801 brought together a number of key elements in Caldas's scientific career. In May he sent in his note regarding the height of the Guadalupe peak to *Correo Curioso*, and although it was an ostensibly anonymous note, his friends in Bogotá seized the opportunity to make Caldas's name known to José Celestino Mutis and bring him into direct contact with the Botanical Expedition. In August, Caldas began a personal correspondence with Mutis that would lead, a year later, to his incorporation as a member of the expedition. And on the last day of the year Caldas met the Prussian naturalist Baron Alexander von Humboldt. This began the only period in which he was to enjoy direct contact with European science.

That same year (1801) Caldas discovered for himself that the boiling point of water varies with atmospheric pressure and used that fact to construct his own scale to make a hypsometric (hypsos: height; metron: measure) thermometer (Fig. 2). This "discovery" is important not only because Caldas's achievement was completely independent, for there was no one in Nueva Granada—not even Mutis—familiar with the principle, but also because the circumstances of Caldas's work and his later discussions with Humboldt illustrate the difficulty of being a scientist without community.

MEASURING MOUNTAINS

In May 1801 Caldas abruptly put aside his astronomical and barometric observations and botanical field trips to concentrate on something new and unsuspected. He announced the matter in an appropriately dramatic way to his friend Arroyo in a letter dated 20 May 1801:

We are on the eve of a discovery that will honor my country. This chapter requires extreme reserve especially as Humboldt and Bonpland approach, since they are capable of penetrating my ideas if we are not careful. . . . I have found, dear friend, the means of finding the altitude of all places using only the thermometer, and with such a degree of precision that it does not differ even by half a line from barometric indications, a precision I would not have expected if experience had not confirmed my ideas.[1]

The road to discovery began by chance for Caldas. He had organized in Popayán a number of field trips with the friends he had interested in

---

[1] Eduardo Posada, ed. *Cartas de Caldas*. Biblioteca de Historia Nacional. Volume 15. Imprenta Nacional. Bogotá. 1917, p. 51.

scientific activities. They would load horses, mules and Indian guides with provisions and Caldas's assorted scientific instruments. During a particular eight-day foray to the Puracé volcano "some five leagues to the east of Popayán," in the company of his friend Antonio Arboleda, Caldas went about one of his common observations. Though interested in knowing if the temperature of snow, found near the mouth of the volcano, varied with latitude, he made no measurement because his thermometer (the last one he had) broke when he forced it into the snow.

When Caldas returned to Popayán he decided to repair it. He had no other choice. Just as he had built his own quadrant, prepared barometer tubes and taken a lens here and there to put together a telescope, he needed to repair this particular thermometer if he was to continue his observations. Once the tube was sealed he began to calibrate the instrument. This was something he clearly had not done before because he simply assumed fixed endpoints. (Caldas worked with the Réamur scale of 0° for the freezing point of water and 80° for the boiling point of water.) When the air temperature of Popayán appeared higher than its common value, and his degree divisions seemed smaller than before, he correctly turned to the boiling point as the source of the problem.

Caldas felt that he was on to something. His own detailed account of how he worked out the solution is given in his "Draft of a New Method . . ." which is presented in translation in Appendix A. I will emphasize here a few selected points.

Caldas had in his possession a text identified as *Física Experimental* by Sigaud de la Fond. There he found a reference to the phenomenon which pointed him in the right direction but did not solve the problem. Acccording to

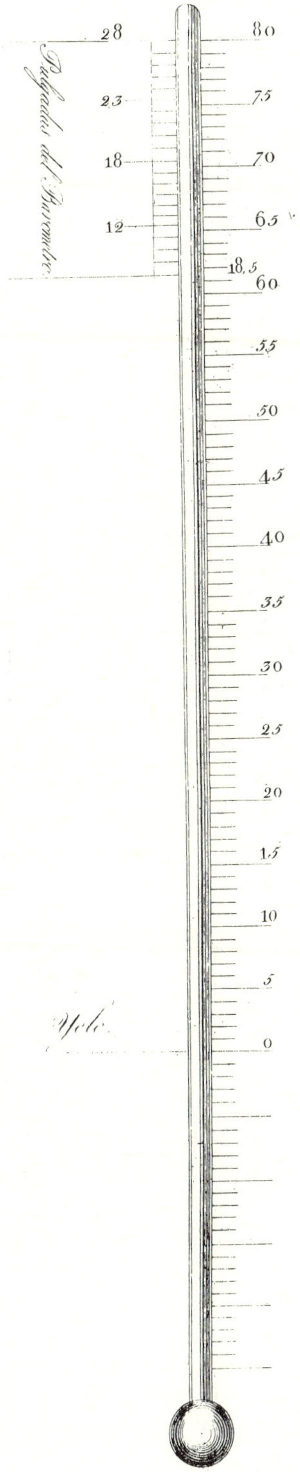

FIGURE 2. Caldas's Hypsometric Thermometer. Reprinted from Eduardo Posada, ed. *Obras de Caldas*. Biblioteca de Historia Nacional. Volume 9. Imprenta Nacional. Bogotá. 1912.

Caldas the text read, "This physicist (a doctor Martine) has discovered that the rise or descent of mercury being of one inch in the barometer, the temperature of boiling water varies something less than two degrees in the Fahrenheit scale."[2]

The only authority available to him, then, clearly identified the boiling point of water as a variable point dependent on the atmospheric pressure. It did not, however, state explicitly any numerical value for the proportion between pressure and temperature, nor did it indicate that this phenomenon could be used to measure altitude. Caldas had, since 1796, made a habit of carrying barometer tubes and thermometers with him wherever he traveled. The implications of his "discovery" were transparently clear and exciting. He immediately understood that altitudes could be measured using a new, hypsometric (a word he never used) thermometer. What remained to be done was to determine the proportionality constant. This he did through a series of observations made at his family's hacienda near Paispamba, south of Popayán and at a somewhat higher altitude. He terminated his work by drawing a scale for his thermometer that gave the atmospheric pressure corresponding to temperatures at the upper end of the scale as shown in Figure 2.

Yet, despite the exhilaration Caldas felt at having come across this new principle and having worked out the means by which it could be applied to measurement, there remained unresolved for him the question of whether or not his discovery was original. Certainly he had independently elaborated his hypsometric scale—he had neither references nor communications with others which dealt with the matter. But was it original? The problem was a nagging one. Caldas expressed the frustration with the hypsometric problem in particular and his situation in general in the following passage from his "Draft of a New Method . . .": "What doubts! How sad is the fate of an American! After much work, if he happens to find something new, the most he can say is—it is not in my books."[3]

HYPSOMETRIC THERMOMETERS BEFORE CALDAS[4]

What Caldas suspected was correct—the variability of the boiling point simply was not in the books he had. At least he had no access to a quantitative discussion of the phenomenon. Had he been less isolated from concurrent European science he would have known that there was much discussion about hypsometric thermometers in the eighteenth century.

The first hypsometric thermometer was constructed by none less than Fahrenheit in 1734 (see Figure 3). Indeed, Fahrenheit's knowledge of the

---

[2] *Obras Completas de Francisco José de Caldas.* Universidad Nacional de Colombia. Imprenta Nacional. Bogotá. 1966, p. 155.

[3] Ibid., 158.

[4] This section follows the discussions found in W. E. Knowles Middleton. *A History of the Thermometer and Its Uses In Meteorology.* The Johns Hopkins Press. Baltimore. 1966.

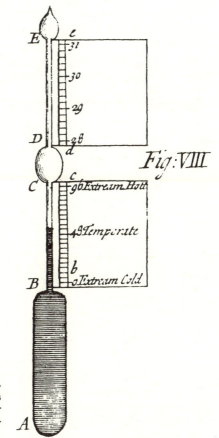

FIGURE 3. Fahrenheit's Hypsometric Thermometer. Reprinted from W. E. Knowles Middleton. *A History of the Thermometer and Its Uses in Meteorology.* The Johns Hopkins Press. Baltimore. 1966.

variability of the boiling point with atmospheric pressure led him to use as an upper fixed point for his thermometers not the boiling point of water, but rather the temperature "of a living man in good health."[5] As shown in the figure Fahrenheit adapted a scale of atmospheric pressure (here in English inches) just as Caldas did nearly seventy years later. The originator of the centigrade scale, Anders Celsius, discussed the boiling point problem in 1742. He preceded Caldas on two counts. Regarding a technical point Celsius noted that the temperature of boiling varies according to the activity or violence of the boiling. Second, he conceived the utility of using this principle to replace the barometer with a thermometer for altitude measurements, thus lightening the load for many an observant traveler.

By the latter part of the eighteenth century the phenomenon was well known enough to be discussed by an ad-hoc committee of the British Royal Society. In 1777 the committee—including Henry Cavendish, Wil-

---

[5] Ibid., 75.

liam Heberden and J. A. DeLuc—considered in detail methods of "adjust-
ing the fixed points of thermometers."[6] With regard to the boiling point
they designed an apparatus for its calibration specifying the value of 29.8
(English) inches of mercury as the standard barometric pressure. In this
case the thermometer was not immersed in the boiling water but rather
held above it, in the steam.

Middleton reports that hypsometers were made and described by
numerous scientists in the late eighteenth and early nineteenth centuries. Adding Caldas's name to the following table gives a perspective
to the matter of which Caldas himself was unaware.

Hypsometer	Year
Fahrenheit	1724
DeLuc	1772
Caldas	1801
Belloni	1805
Wollaston	1817
Regnault	1845

HUMBOLDT'S VERDICT

Caldas was desperately anxious to confirm the originality of his work.
And fortuitously, if not miraculously, the year 1801 gave him a first-rate
opportunity. Baron Alexander von Humboldt, Caldas's contemporary at
32 years of age arrived in the Viceroyalty of Nueva Granada as part of
his round-the-world voyage to the colonies of the Spanish empire.
Humboldt's trip through Nueva Granada and his influence on Caldas in
other matters will be dealt with in the following chapter. But, to complete
the discussion of Caldas's hypsometric thermometer, we must at this
point jump ahead to take note of what the Prussian was able to tell the
Granadian. In Caldas's correspondence for the latter half of 1801, the
matter of the boiling point casts a constant shadow. It was not always in
the forefront—Caldas began his correspondence with Mutis that year
without mention of it—and in August was obliged to travel from Popayán
to Quito to represent his family's claim for an inheritance. But throughout this period he protected and sheltered his invention, for it was an
accomplishment he felt was truly his own.

When Caldas first announced his discovery to his friend Arroyo, in
May 1801, he already knew of the arrival of Humboldt and was concerned with protecting his priority on the subject lest Humboldt be
"capable of penetrating my ideas." It seems clear that initially Caldas
thought it was possible that only the fact of boiling point variability be
known. That is, he had no indication that his observations had been
anticipated on the following points: a) that there exists an exact relation
between atmospheric pressure and the boiling point of water; b) that the

---

[6] Ibid., 127.

boiling point can be used to measure altitudes; and c) that a thermometer equipped with an appropriate scale can completely replace the barometer for the determination of pressure and, hence, altitude.

So it was with great consternation that Caldas received Arroyo's note that Humboldt had measured in Bogotá the boiling point of water:

The news you have sent me that Baron von Humboldt plunges the thermometer in boiling water and rectifies the barometric height makes me think with cause that the law of the elevation of the liquor of the thermometer in water is known to him and that he knows how to apply that to the calculation of altitudes. How certain it is that we are two centuries behind Europe![7]

It was clear then that point a) above had slipped from Caldas's grasp and, perhaps, b) and c) as well. Yet Caldas maintained control and decided to wait for a closer look:

However I do not yet consider my thoughts to be null. Let us wait for this wise Baron, let us probe the principles and finalities with which he observes the heat of water and then I will tell you if there is something new to my observations and our theory, or if I have only come upon that which was known in Europe many years ago.[8]

Caldas had taken up residence in Quito in connection with his family's legal affairs. He decided to cease all work on the boiling point problem until he could speak with Humboldt. The baron's trip would lead to Popayán, Caldas's hometown, in November. Caldas wrote to his friend Arboleda, who was in Popayán, cautioning him not to reveal any of Caldas's work to Humboldt. Instead, Caldas instructed Arboleda to listen to Humboldt and take "all of the possible advantages from this occasion, perhaps the only of its kind in our lifetime."

Although the two naturalists met on New Year's Eve 1801, Caldas did not enter into discussion of the matter until March 1802. Undoubtedly he wanted to gain the baron's confidence, to take his measure before presenting his discovery. Furthermore, Caldas was very timid on first approach and the importance he assigned to the problem must have increased his wariness.

Humboldt did not, however, completely solve the problem.[9] The baron referred Caldas to the work of Saussure[10] stating that Saussure did indeed measure altitudes using boiling water but that he used a linear relation between temperature and altitude. This was in error since pressure varies exponentially with height. Humboldt was critical of Saussure's method and told Caldas that "the method of this physicist has been abandoned because of its inexactness."[11]

---

7 Eduardo Posada, ed. *Cartas de Caldas*. Biblioteca de Historia Nacional. Volume 15. Imprenta Nacional. Bogotá. 1917, p. 95.

8 Ibid., 95.

9 This part of the discussion is based wholly on Caldas's version of events.

10 Horace Benedict de Saussure (b. 1740, d. 1799). Swiss naturalist.

11 Eduardo Posada, ed. *Cartas de Caldas*. Biblioteca de Historia Nacional. Volume 15. Imprenta Nacional. Bogotá. 1917, p. 140.

The exact exchange of ideas on the hypsometric principle between Caldas and Humboldt is even less certain because in a short memoir that Caldas wrote to Mutis he insists that Humboldt later retracted his initial comments. According to Caldas the baron reviewed his notes and found that the work of Saussure refers to air temperature and not the temperature of boiling water. This change of events gave Caldas a renewed claim to priority.

Caldas wrote two memoirs on the subject and commented on it frequently throughout 1801 and 1802 in letters to Arroyo and Arboleda. Yet he cites Humboldt only on the method of Saussure. It would seem that the baron was unaware in 1802 of the development of hypsometric thermometers discussed in the previous section. Humboldt used the method sparingly, sticking mainly to barometric measurements of pressure. Indeed, the principle of boiling point variability seems to have been, in Humboldt's mind, an experimental fact in need of further investigation.

Humboldt did issue a later comment, a rather noncommittal one, on the matter of boiling water and Caldas wrote in his *Physical Sketch of the Equatorial Andes:*

In the course of my travels I have performed many experiments on the boiling point of water in the Andean peaks. I hope to publish these along with others executed by Mr. Caldas, native of Popayán, a distinguished physicist who has consecrated his efforts with an unequaled passion to astronomy and many branches of natural history.[12]

Humboldt was not, then, the complete authority on European science that Caldas had imagined. Why was the baron unaware of the development of hypsometric thermometers? Perhaps he simply had not taken time, or did not have the interest, to investigate the matter prior to his journey to the New World. Had he not come across the scientists familiar with the subject? He seems to have been more familiar with French science than with the work of the English. The answers to these questions lie beyond the scope of the present study, but it is important to note that what Humboldt told Caldas was all that the latter was to know of the state of the matter in Europe.

Based on his discussions with Humboldt, Caldas concluded that he in fact had worked out the application of the boiling point principle to altitude in an original way. As he wrote to Arroyo in March 1802:

Saussure has preceded me in the theory, but the formula is mine as is the glory of having resolved this physical problem in an elegant manner; and furthermore, that my method, absolutely different from that of Saussure is so exact that the largest differences in the results are no more than 1½ lines, an exactness which has not been achieved by Mr. Saussure nor any other European. . . . Now you can congratulate me. I know what is known in Europe on the matter and if I was

---

12 Alexander von Humboldt. *Ideas Para Una Geografia De Las Plantas Mas Un Cuadro De La Naturaleza De Los Paises Tropicales.* Jardín Botánico 'José Celestino Mutis.' Bogotá. 1985, p. 98.

able to arrive at the fundamental theory by way of my miserable books, I have elaborated the calculation via a different route and have given the method a degree of perfection not to be found in Europe.[13]

Caldas continued his work on the hypsometric principle, but, it gradually gave way in importance to the problems of plant geography, the cinchona tree and other facets of botany and geography. His work with the Botanical Expedition expanded his interests, so the solution of the boiling point problem was an accomplishment whose chapter soon came to an end.

---

[13] Eduardo Posada, ed. *Cartas de Caldas*. Biblioteca de Historia Nacional. Volume 15. Imprenta Nacional. Bogotá. 1917, p. 140.

III. HUMBOLDT IN TRANSIT

The end of the eighteenth century found new ideas filtering through to the populace of Nueva Granada. No longer did the Inquisition control the intellectual climate. That Mutis had won the case for teaching Copernicanism was evidence of the popularity of the "new philosophy." The Spanish crown could not control the flow of political news—there was great interest in the American and French revolutions—and in fact it had begun to support the investigation and dissemination of scientific ideas. People were curious, impatient for news and anxious for greater contact with the personalities and ideas to be found outside of the Spanish Empire.

So it was that the passage of the naturalist Baron Alexander von Humboldt, accompanied by the French botanist Aime Bonpland, through Nueva Granada in 1801 and 1802 took on a significance beyond that which might have been expected a generation earlier. News of the traveler's arrival moved quickly from Cartagena to Bogotá to Popayán to Quito and back. The entire viceroyalty seemed to be in constant communication about the Europeans.

Rumors spread. Humboldt traveled with a priest—not so, it was Bonpland with short-cropped hair and black attire. Humboldt maintained a mistress—not so, the woman was mistress to Louis de Rieux, commissioner for quinine production who accompanied Humboldt and Bonpland up the Magdalena River. Humboldt spoke no Spanish—not so, he had become a fluent speaker in the first part of his trip, through Venezuela, a year earlier.

This was Europe come to America, and the occasion was momentous. This was a cultural event—a chance to compare, to inquire, to criticize.

Humboldt had planned, though, a primarily scientific expedition. And in this context the moment was even more opportune. At thirty years of age and already a well-known figure in Europe, he had embarked on an ambitious journey which has been called "the scientific discovery of America." José Celestino Mutis was nearly seventy years old. He knew that his life's work—the Flora of Bogotá—would not be completed before his death. Mutis was anxious to leave his reputation and his work established with the scientific community of Europe. And Caldas, the scientist in search of community was, in 1801, a young and talented man. Yet he knew that he was at a crossroad and that his future as a scientist depended on choosing the right path. The trajectories of these stellar figures for science in Nueva Granada were to be brought together in 1801 and 1802 in brilliant conjunction.

20

FIGURE 4. Portrait of Mutis. Reprinted from Alfredo D. Bateman. *El Observatorio Astronómico de Bogotá*. Universidad Nacional de Colombia. Bogotá. 1953.

FROM BERLIN TO BOGOTÁ

When Friedrich Wilhelm Heinrich Alexander von Humboldt arrived in Spain near the end of 1798 to obtain permission for a planned trip to the Spanish colonies, he had already established a reputation for himself in European scientific circles. Humboldt, who was born in Berlin in 1769, had a wide and varied background. Among his fields of interest were mining, geography, astronomy, geomagnetism, vulcanism, galvanism and botany. He had also traveled extensively throughout Europe. It was, however, the inheritance that he received upon his mother's death that gave him the opportunity to organize a trip to America.

Humboldt was joined in Paris by the botanist Aime Bonpland, four years younger than the baron. Bonpland's expenses were covered by Humboldt. The two voyagers set sail from Spain on 5 June 1799 and arrived in what is now Venezuela on 16 July. They spent a year and a half traveling in Venezuelan territory, measuring latitudes, longitudes and altitudes, observing flora and fauna, and investigating Indian cultures. They followed the Orinoco River deep into the tropical rain forest returning in December 1800 to the coast where they left for Cuba.

Humboldt had planned a trip around the world stopping first in Spain's American colonies and later the Philippines. He hoped to reach the Pacific coast at Guayaquil (Ecuador) and continue on to Mexico and Asia. The travelers did not choose, though, to cross the Isthmus of Panama. They headed instead for the route through Nueva Granada while sending the heavier part of their cargo across Panama to Guayaquil. The reason for their detour was straightforward. Humboldt wanted to meet with Mutis in Bogotá.

The Europeans first stop in Nueva Granada was the port city of Cartagena. Here they were received by José Ignacio de Pombo, a native of Popayán, who was a businessman and a member of the Consulado de Cartagena, an organization charged with the promotion of commerce and development in the viceroyalty. Pombo took his guests to his country house in Turbo, which he had purchased from Mutis's patron, Archbishop Caballero y Gongora. Pombo maintained an active correspondence with Mutis and was well-informed on events both inside and outside the viceroyalty.

While in Cartagena Humboldt established contact with the Fidalgo expedition which had been commissioned to map the Caribbean coast. They exchanged information on geographical positions and measurements, Humboldt being especially interested in the calibration of his chronometer before heading inland.

Humboldt and Bonpland left Cartagena via the Magdalena River in company of the aforementioned Rieux. The trip to Bogotá carried them first up the river to the town of Honda. This part of the journey took forty days. The tropical climate took its toll on Bonpland who contracted malaria. Humboldt curiously enough seems to have thrived in the tropics. Throughout their passage through Nueva Granada, Bonpland's health was delicate; Humboldt's superb. From Honda the trip to Bogotá was made by mule, passing through rugged terrain and extreme changes in altitude.

In Bogotá the citizenry awaited anxiously. Humboldt was pleased and surprised with the reception. He wrote to his brother, "Our arrival in Santa Fe [Bogotá] was like a triumphal march. The archbishop had sent us his coach which had arrived with the notables of the city. We were

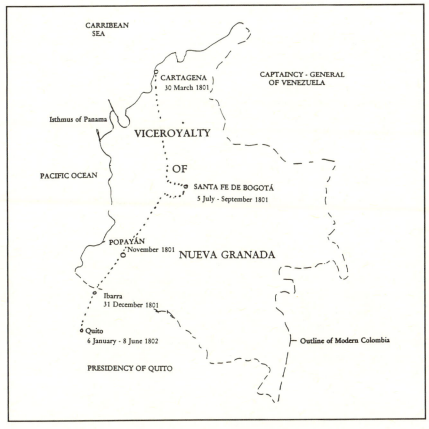

MAP 2. Humboldt's Route through Nueva Granada.

served lunch some two miles from there and we entered in the company of more than sixty persons on horseback."[1]

The travelers arrived on 15 July 1801 and although they hoped to continue quickly to the Pacific coast, it was necessary to delay time enough for Bonpland to convalesce from his illness.

They spoke at length with Mutis who had prepared a house for them to stay in. He gave them complete access to the works of the Botanical Expedition and to his personal library as well. Humboldt later declared the library to be second only to the personal library of Joseph Banks in London. Mutis was interested in giving a clear and positive impression of the Botanical Expedition and the Flora of Bogotá for the travelers to take with them on their return. In this Mutis succeeded judging from Humboldt's comment to Antonio Cavanilles in a letter dated April 1803, "He [Mutis] is now in his old age but his finished works and those that he is preparing for posterity are stunning. It is admirable that a single man has been capable of conceiving and executing such a vast plan."[2]

[1] Hermann A. Schumacher. *Mutis, un Forjador de la Cultura.* Traducción de Ernesto Guhl. Empresa Colombiana de Petroleos, ECOPETROL. Bogotá. 1984, p. 239.
[2] Enrique Perez Arbelaez, ed. *Alejandro Humboldt en Colombia.* Instituto Colombiano de Cultura. Bogotá. 1982, p. 256.

In addition, Mutis gave to Humboldt a collection of 100 drawings of plants to be included in his proposed Flora. For his part, Humboldt gave Mutis a map of the Magdalena River drawn from the astronomical measurements made during the trip from Cartagena.

Humboldt, who impressed all he met as being energetic, made good use of his extended stay in Bogotá. While Bonpland recovered, the baron visited, measured and described the nearby Tequendama Falls; acquainted himself with local Indian lore and language; studied the mining of salt at Zipaquira and wrote a report on this for the viceroy[3] at once fulfilling his obligation to provide technical advice to the Spanish crown in exchange for his travel permit and demonstrating his expertise on mining; gave a second copy of his map of the Magdalena River to the viceroy; studied the reports of earlier viceroys to learn of the economic and social history of the colony; and continued his geographic observations, determining the position of Bogotá, the heights of the Monserrate and Guadalupe peaks and, as noted, the effect of altitude on the boiling point of water. When Bonpland improved, the travelers pressed on toward the Pacific. They left Bogotá at the beginning of September. Humboldt described the occasion, "The following day we left with eleven pack animals. The farewell in Mutis' house was emotional. The old man treated us with generosity and kindness. He provided us with provisions that three strong mules were scarcely capable of carrying."[4]

For the next two months the Europeans suffered again the rigors of travel across the high Andean peaks to Quindio and later through the Cauca Valley until their arrival on 4 November 1801 to Caldas's home town of Popayán. Humboldt wrote:

The situation of Popayán is delicious. A pleasant landscape, beautiful vegetation, even climate, the most majestic thunder one has ever heard, the productions of the tropics in front of the snow-capped Andean peaks; the mixture of the grand and the beautiful, these varied contrasts, which the knowing hand of the Almighty has placed in perfect harmony, fill the soul with the greatest and most interesting images.[5]

But Caldas was not in Popayán. He had been pressed into active duty as a lawyer once again. Although the information given by Caldas is sketchy, it is clear that he became involved in litigation regarding an inheritance that was to be received by his parents but was disputed by the family of his first cousin, Camilo Torres. When Caldas won the first round in Popayán his relatives lodged an appeal in Quito. So despite his interest in meeting with the European, Caldas had left Popayán in August.

Furthermore, Caldas's friend, relative, correspondent and confidant, Antonio Arboleda was not in the city. Arboleda was attending matters

---

[3] Caldas obtained a copy of this report via his friend Arroyo.

[4] Hermann A. Schumacher. *Mutis, un Forjador de la Cultura*. Traducción de Ernesto Guhl. Empresa Colombiana de Petroleos, ECOPETROL. Bogotá. 1984, p. 178.

[5] Ibid., 241.

at his family's hacienda. No one was available to give Humboldt an account of Caldas's work. (Except for the discovery of the boiling point phenomenon which was to be kept secret in any case. Caldas was extremely careful in instructing his friends to not allow the travelers information which might jeopardize his possible priority.)

Yet the baron was clearly well-informed about Caldas. So when he met with Caldas's father, Humboldt read with interest Caldas's notebook of observations. Especially noteworthy for the Prussian was Caldas's observation of an occultation of one of the Galilean satellites and subsequent calculation of longitude. It agreed exactly with his own.

Humboldt was more than curious about this unknown Granadian. He had seen Caldas's note in *Correo Curioso*, had been acquainted with Caldas's circle of friends in Bogotá, and had seen the notebooks and calculations of a man who must properly be described as a working scientist. Furthermore, Caldas's work using astronomical observations for geographical measurements was in tone with Humboldt's program of observations throughout his journey. Accordingly, Humboldt wrote in his diary, without having met Caldas, the following:

This Caldas is a prodigy at astronomy. Born in the darkness of Popayán he has been able to teach himself, fashion barometers, sectors, quarter circles, measure latitudes with gnomons of fifteen to twenty feet. I have seen the corresponding latitudes measured with these instruments which only differ from four to five lines. What would such a spirit have done in a cultured nation and what could not be expected of him if he did not have to do everything for himself.[6]

This judgment more than anything else was to secure for Caldas esteem among his contemporaries and his place in Colombian history.

The Europeans spent the month of November in Popayán. They made various excursions to study the flora of the region. Humboldt wrote a description of the Vinagre River which they observed on a trip to the same Puracé Volcano which started Caldas on his work on the boiling point of water. But once again they felt the need to press on, this time to Quito.

Caldas had grown impatient. He decided to leave Quito and meet the travelers in the town of Ibarra. Caldas wrote to a friend on 21 December 1801:

Baron von Humboldt is very close to us. He left Popayán on November 27th and I find myself hurried with the trip to Ibarra. I want to meet, alone and free of the mass of adulators, this great man. I hope to show him my observations on all subjects and receive sage commentary about them. What well-founded expectations have I to become an astronomer![7]

The next day Caldas left Quito. Humboldt and Bonpland spent Christmas 1801 in the city of Pasto. And on 31 December 1801, at 11:00 a.m., in Ibarra Caldas and Humboldt shook hands.

---

6 Eduardo Posada, ed. *Cartas de Caldas*. Biblioteca de Historia Nacional. Volume 15. Imprenta Nacional. Bogotá. 1917, p. 126.

7 Ibid., 113.

Scientists at Work

That same day the discussion turned to Caldas's work. In his letters he cites these comments by Humboldt: "I have seen the precious works of yours in astronomy and geography. They were shown to me in Popayán. I have seen [astronomical] altitudes measured with such precision that the greatest difference [with mine] does not pass four seconds [of arc]"[8] and, ". . . your father, without your consent, has shown me a book of notes, in which I found an observation of the occultation of the first satellite of Jupiter and calculation; and it gives the same longitude as my chronometer—read for yourself."[9]

This was clearly the beginning of a mutually beneficial relationship. Humboldt had been traveling since 1799 and found in Caldas the first person with whom he could compare astronomical and geographical observations. During his stay in Bogotá he dealt with Mutis about the Flora Bogotana, the cinchona problem and other matters related to the Botanical Expedition. But Mutis was neither a particularly active nor a very careful observer with the telescope and barometer. Here Caldas was undoubtedly superior. Furthermore, Caldas had made many observations that Humboldt was anxious to see.

Caldas gladly showed the baron his astronomical notebooks. He also presented his map of Timaná, "I showed him my map of Timaná and another piece that I made in 1796 from Tocaima to Neiva; so that joining these with those of the baron we have a map of the entire Magdalena [River]."[10]

Humboldt asked for a copy and later commented, "I have seen many maps in the offices of Caracas, Cartagena and Santa Fe [Bogotá]; and the only one that deserves that name, the only one determined astronomically is that of Timaná."[11]

Humboldt also made note of Caldas's determination of altitudes by barometric measurements. And, later in March, Caldas presented the altitudes determined by the boiling point method.

For Caldas the encounter was exhilarating. Here was the opportunity to get a clear idea of what he knew and what he did not know; of how good his books were; of how lacking his knowledge of recent developments was; of how good a scientist he was. By the time they arrived in Quito, Humboldt had given Caldas access to his notebooks. They held numerous discussions on scientific topics and they took measurements together. Some things were quite new for Caldas. For example, he wrote, "Until now I had believed that negative electricity was a lack of electricity, but now we have escaped this error. They are two distinct fluids that have equal and opposite properties. What a paradox! But, such a well-established physical truth!"[12]

---

8 Ibid., 115.
9 Ibid., 115.
10 Ibid., 116.
11 Ibid., 116.
12 Ibid., 128.

FIGURE 5. Portrait of Humboldt, APS Archives.

On other matters Humboldt informed Caldas of refinements in methodology. He showed Caldas new methods for calculating altitudes from barometric measurements, and instructed him in the use of various meteorological instruments.

With regard to astronomy Humboldt trained Caldas in the use of the octant; gave him tables of astronomical refractions and a star catalog; and discussed computational methods with him. Caldas's progress was such that he wrote, "In astronomy I do not recognize myself. A thick veil of difficulty has vanished from in front of my eyes and, as I had many observations and works nearly finished, only the hand of a master was missing to give them the final touch. . . ."[13]

In Quito the Europeans were hosted by the Marques de Selvalegre, Juan Pio Montufar, who was a friend and associate of their host in Cartagena, Jose Ignacio de Pombo. Montufar invited the travelers to his hacienda at Chillo. Caldas accompanied them, staying in the same room with Bonpland. They spent 37 days in February and March 1802 working near Chillo. In Caldas's account of this period he mentions field trips for plant specimens with Bonpland; measuring by trigonometric means the height of the Pichincha Volcano with Humboldt; the programmed dissection of a llama; and Humboldt's climbing of the peak at Antisana (Caldas did not go along, perhaps because of illness).

Also during their stay in Chillo Caldas asked Humboldt to suggest a list of scientific instruments that could be purchased in Europe. The idea for this purchase came from Caldas's friend, relative and first benefactor, Manuel Maria Arboleda. Caldas followed up on the idea. One continuous thread running through Caldas's scientific life is his acute awareness of the inadequacy of the books and instruments available in the viceroyalty. So he must have seized the moment which brought together his benefactor's generosity and the presence of Humboldt's authority.

Caldas later sent to Arboleda a long list,[14] including prices, as a result of his discussions with the baron. The list included thermometers, pyrometers, barometers, weights and measures (meters, toises, feet), electrometers, hygrometers, magnets, sextants, octants, a Dollond achromatic telescope, compound microscope, lenses, two seven-foot long telescopes, theodolite, chronometer, and collections of minerals and insects, among others. The total cost initially was $10,000 pesos but was later limited to $5,000 pesos. The instruments were to be ordered through friends of Humboldt—the astronomer Maskelyne in London, Lalande in Paris, and the astronomer Brodhagen in Hamburg. Humboldt provided letters of recommendation. These letters were sent to Arboleda in Popayán who sent $5,000 pesos to Camilo Torres in Bogotá, to be forwarded later to Pombo in Cartagena. But the purchase was never carried out, most likely owing to the subsequent falling out between Humboldt and Caldas.

Finally it must be noted that the greatest part of the time spent in Chillo, Caldas dealt with botanical matters. The influence of Humboldt and especially Bonpland on Caldas's development as a botanist will be dealt with in the next chapter, but it is worth mentioning at this point that both Caldas and Humboldt were keenly interested in the distribution of plant species with altitude. Certainly during their field trips and discussions at Chillo they must have dealt with the subject.

---

[13] Ibid., 118.
[14] Jorge Arias de Greiff. "Algo Mas Sobre Caldas y Humboldt." *Boletín de la Sociedad Geográfica de Colombia.* Volume 27. Number 101. 1970.

What Might Have Been

For Caldas science, whether astronomy, geography or botany, was what interested him most. Even further, it could be said that science was his only passion, captivating him in a way that neither his wife nor the revolution were able to do. That this was so is seen in his letters less than a month after meeting Humboldt and Bonpland. Caldas found himself in scientific heaven, a kind of ecstatic daydream which he did not want to end. In a letter dated 21 January 1802 to Arroyo, Caldas wrote: "Who may know if as with a bolt of lightening we are illuminated for an instant only to fall into an even deeper darkness?"[15]

Caldas already had a solution. He would continue on with the Europeans for the rest of their trip through the Americas. (Although Caldas limited his proposal to America, I think that there can be no doubt that he harbored ambitions for continuing on to Europe.) This would be a first-rate apprenticeship that would make him a first-rate scientist. And, although Caldas usually showed himself timid in his relationships, in this case, for the sake of his science, he launched an offensive. To Arroyo he continued:

My friend would there be some way to find support at least to continue in America with Humboldt? Would not Señor Mutis, the protector of the sciences in the viceroyalty, have some influence with the Viceroy, so that I might be able to travel for some time with this sage?[16]

Caldas came up square against a fundamental problem for any scientist at any time—funding. Another facet of Caldas's scientific career of importance is his activity as a fund raiser in a place and at a time when there were no funds for scientists, save those deemed available by the Spanish crown, half a world away. Beginning with his friend and relative Arboleda, Caldas demonstrated a marked ability to convince prospective benefactors to support his work. As with the need for community, Caldas seems to have had an instinctive understanding of the role of funding in the scientific enterprise.

Initially Caldas centered his attention on the viceroy and the Consulado de Cartagena of which José Ignacio de Pombo was a member. He sent letters on the matter to Arroyo, Miguel Pombo, Camilo Torres and Mutis. By the time Caldas returned to Quito from Chillo, Arroyo had hit on a different plan. Friends and relatives would each subscribe a share of Caldas's expenses. Caldas was elated.

And then, events took a dramatic turn. Caldas received from Mutis a letter (on 3 April 1802) wherein Mutis stated his willingness to support the plan. He sent a stipend along with the letter and stated further that he (Mutis) had sent a letter of recommendation to Humboldt in Caldas's favor. Armed with what he felt to be the answer to his prayers Caldas

---

[15] Eduardo Posada, ed. *Cartas de Caldas*. Biblioteca de Historia Nacional. Volume 15. Imprenta Nacional. Bogotá. 1917, p. 117.
[16] Ibid., 117.

rushed to Humboldt's residence only to find the Prussian unusually reserved. Humboldt claimed at first that he had received no such letter from Mutis. But Caldas insisted, forcing Humboldt to confess: "My friend, I have lied to you. Mutis has written me at length on the matter, but I have resolved to continue alone and did not want you to be afflicted by my decision."[17]

Yet this was not true. Humboldt indeed was going to add a companion to his traveling party. This was Carlos Montufar, son of the Europeans' host, who was to accompany them not only throughout America but also to travel with them to Europe.

Caldas did not take it well. His letters to his friends and to Mutis no longer contained limitless, even excessive, praise of the baron, but rather an uncontrolled wrath. Why did Humboldt not accede to the wishes of Caldas and Mutis? Caldas was sure the answer lay with the difference in his and Humboldt's personalities. Among Caldas's extended commentary on the matter are the following:

[To Mutis on 6 April 1802]

The personalities of Humboldt and Caldas are very different. The former possesses a liveliness that borders on restlessness; loquacious, lover of society and amusement. The latter with a background of activity maintains a certain degree of slowness in his operations; taciturn, with a somewhat austere lifestyle and lover of privacy, with a frequently tranquil expression, rarely smiling, neither jumps, sings, runs or fights. This is the origin of his refusal say what he might Baron von Humboldt.[18]

[To Mutis on 21 April]

How different is the conduct of the baron in Quito from what he showed in Santa Fe [Bogotá] and Popayán! . . . The baron enters this Babylon, becomes friends with a few dissolute, obscene youths; they drag him to the houses where tainted love reigns; this shameful passion takes control of his heart and blinds this young sage to a point that one is incapable of believing.[19]

And when Humboldt left Quito in June with Montufar in the group, Caldas unleashed his cruelest and most insinuating comment: "Baron von Humboldt left here on the eighth [June 1802] in company of Bonpland and of his Adonis who does not interfere with his trip as does Caldas."[20]

Certainly Caldas was guilty of a lack of self-control and needless exaggeration. But what is there to his charges? First of all, it must be said that Caldas's plan was eminently reasonable, well-developed and that he had taken steps to assure its success. Thus, the baron's rejection rightly stunned not only Caldas, but Mutis as well who wrote to Humboldt in May:

---

[17] Ibid., 149.
[18] Ibid., 149.
[19] Ibid., 153.
[20] Ibid., 168.

What is this my dear Baron? What! Will a proposal made with the greatest sincerity and frankness be capable of altering our solid friendship? Is it my fault that Caldas has grown so enthused with the illustrious Baron that he wants to follow you through the two Americas? Could I have proceeded with greater frankness than that expressed in my letter having sent for you to read the answer and draft of funds to Caldas? And would not my real intention be to nominate a student I thought would be to your liking? Break, your grace, then, your silence and as if nothing had happened, continue your grace in correspondence with your dear friend.[21]

That Humboldt would decide against Caldas is not immediately reasonable. Several suggestions have been offered—the clash of personalities, the extra expenses that Caldas's inclusion would cause and the presence of Caldas as a scientific competitor. There is no way to read the Prussian's mind from this vantage point, but it is worth commenting the way a mix of elements may have led to his decision.

It is my opinion that from Humboldt's point of view Caldas simply did not fit and that each of the above mentioned suggestions may have some validity. Insinuations of the relation with Montufar aside, the fact is that he traveled with Humboldt and Bonpland to Europe. I think that it is not unlikely that Humboldt felt a certain obligation to include him following the handsome treatment given by the Marques de Selvalegre. What father of the epoch would not have wished for his son to study in Europe? In addition, the travelers spent more time in Quito (Chillo included) than in any other part of the viceroyalty.

As for the social factor, Humboldt did make the following comment: "Despite the horrors and dangers with which nature has surrounded them, the inhabitants of Quito are happy, lively, friendly. Their city breathes luxury and voluptuousness, and perhaps there reigns in no other part a more decided and general inclination for entertainment."[22]

On this point, then, Caldas may be given a certain degree of credence. With regard to economics, the trip cost Humboldt dearly. Bonpland's expenses were already being covered by the baron. Given the delays in communications, the age of Mutis and the political uncertainty in Europe, Humboldt may well have reasoned that Caldas's supporters were well-intentioned but that the risk was his.

Finally, the notion that Caldas was a competitor has its merits. Certainly both were developing their ideas regarding plant geography (see Chapter V) at the same time and they coincided in many other areas of interest. Furthermore, Caldas was more methodical and cautious in his operations. Humboldt tended to accept second-hand commentary to a greater degree and maintained notes on a much wider variety of topics.

---

21 Guillermo Hernandez de Alba, ed. *Archivo Epistolar Del Sabio Naturalista Don José Celestino Mutis*. Four Volumes. Instituto Colombiano de Cultura Hispánica. Bogotá. 1983. Volume II, p. 175.
    22 Enrique Perez Arbelaez, ed. *Alejandro Humboldt En Colombia*. Instituto Colombiano de Cultura. Bogotá. 1982, p. 245.

Yet in Caldas's mind I think there was no doubt that Humboldt was the master and he the pupil, despite later comments critical of Humboldt's methodology.

Rather, I think that Humboldt saw in Caldas's meticulousness, in his insistence to ask about everything that came to mind and his single-mindedness with regard to science – to the exclusion of social events – an element that conflicted with the style of Humboldt's excursion. Humboldt had his way of doing things. Caldas's manner, and here I mean scientific manner, was different enough to complicate what was already a difficult and expensive project.

Life Continues

Despite the drama surrounding their conflict, the two scientists slowly patched up their differences. Indeed, many years later Caldas referred enthusiastically to Humboldt's writings, and Humboldt adulated Caldas when he had occasion to mention him. This, then, is not an epilogue to their relation for there will be reference to Humboldt farther on, but an opportunity to mention a few points of interest prior to and following the Europeans' departure from Quito.

Having made his decision to continue on to Peru, Humboldt offered to sell Caldas his quarter circle, made by the English instrument-maker John Bird. Perhaps it was clear that the long list of instruments would not be purchased. Perhaps he needed the money. Certainly it was a gesture of reconciliation. Humboldt charged $300 pesos as the original price plus $100 pesos for its transport to America. It had to be brought from the port city of Guayaquil where it awaited with the heavier parts of Humboldt's equipment that had been brought via Panama and by sea along the Pacific coast.

As has been pointed out, it would have been difficult for Caldas to find a better instrument. Caldas knew that and managed to raise the funds to buy it and put it immediately to use to observe the summer solstice of 1802.

Humboldt also asked Caldas to join him on a field trip to the Pichincha Volcano. Caldas declined, but on a second occasion accepted. They climbed up past the snow line. It seemed that a spirit of comradeship began to grow anew. Caldas described the outing:

I have seen the baron on the verge of extinction. . . . An Indian who was in front of him saved this precious life from death. I followed close behind the baron and the two of us were the first to reach the peak. This traveler is courageous, but I saw him tremble at the edge of the rocks. I shared the danger with him, no less frightened. I helped make the barometric measurements and then descended. . . .[23]

---

[23] Eduardo Posada, ed. *Cartas de Caldas*. Biblioteca de Historia Nacional. Volume 15. Imprenta Nacional. Bogotá. 1917, p. 168.

Later, when the Europeans arrived in Peru, the two exchanged letters. Caldas wrote to Humboldt of geographic measurements, barometric observations and other matters. But principally he wrote of his observation of the transit of Mercury in front of the Sun on 9 November 1802. Caldas observed the final two contact points. Humboldt had suggested the event. And since the Fidalgo expedition in Cartagena also observed the transit, this may be taken as a high water mark for astronomy during this period.

With the departure of Humboldt, one period of Caldas's career comes to an end. Interested principally in astronomy and geography at first, he was now to begin a period dedicated to botanical investigations. The scientist in search of community had come to know European science. He would soon become a member of the Botanical Expedition. But Caldas would not be just another member; he would enter as the heir apparent to Mutis, the most important scientist the viceroyalty had known. And finally, Caldas had come to know himself, to take his own measure. He had gained confidence in his abilities, awareness of his weaknesses and fortified his desire to continue on as a scientist.

Caldas concluded: "I have worked more in four months in Quito than in many years in Popayán."[24]

---

[24] Ibid., 163.

SECTION TWO

WITH THE BOTANICAL EXPEDITION
1802–1806

Once his dream of traveling with Humboldt and Bonpland had vanished, Caldas enthusiastically accepted the offer of Mutis to become a member of the Botanical Expedition. Since his travels as an itinerant merchant, Caldas had taken an interest in the lush vegetation of America. Through his correspondence with Mutis and the friendly instruction of Bonpland, Caldas acquainted himself with the formal elements of botany.

Caldas remained in the Presidency of Quito (modern Ecuador) until the end of 1805. He traveled extensively collecting plants, scaling volcanos, measuring latitudes and retracing the path of the French expedition to the equator. He had suggested to Mutis his own program of investigation. Owing to uncertainties in communications and Mutis's failing health Caldas was left largely on his own. The Granadian demonstrated a surprising facility for gaining patronage for his work. During this period he received support from Mutis, from the merchant and member of the Consulate of Cartagena, José Ignacio de Pombo, and from the President of Quito, Baron Carondelet.

Caldas independently developed the notion of plant geography—the distribution of plant species depending on altitude. His studies mirrored those of Humboldt whose own work undoubtedly spurred Caldas's enthusiasm for the subject. Caldas's observations and travels from tropical rain forest to snow-capped mountains peaks laid the basis for continuing work on phytogeography which he later regarded as his most important intellectual effort.

Mutis meanwhile was more concerned with bringing order to the study of the cinchona tree, whose bark is used to produce quinine. Because of a bitter priority dispute and some unfortunate errors, the cinchona problem was of overriding importance to Mutis in establishing his reputation for posterity. The perceived urgency of the problem led Mutis and Pombo to pressure Caldas to suspend his own pursuits and travel to Loja, reputedly home of the most effective species of cinchona. Caldas complied, completed the mission and then traveled from Quito to Bogotá with an extensive herbarium, the only collection which the Botanical Expedition received from Ecuador.

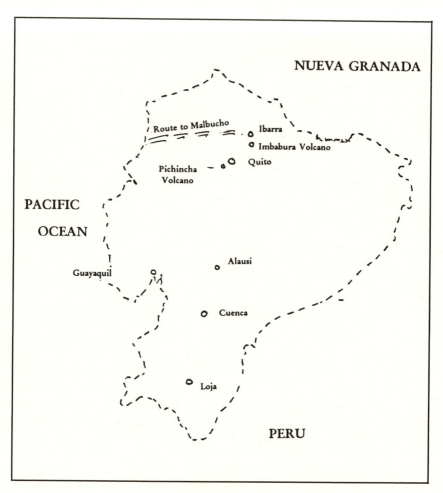

NUEVA GRANADA

Route to Malbucho

Ibarra

Imbabura Volcano

Pichincha
Volcano

Quito

PACIFIC

OCEAN

Guayaquil

Alausi

Cuenca

Loja

PERU

MAP 3.
With the Botanical Expedition: 1802–1806.

IV. BECOMING A BOTANIST

Caldas spent some five years in and around his native Popayán pursuing a scientific career based on his own instincts and a few "miserable" books. A scientist in search of community, he soon found that progress in science is made with reference to that which is already known and on problems which the community finds worthwhile. On both these counts there was little more to go on than the dusty memoirs of La Condamine and Bouger (see Chapter I). Caldas's choice of astronomy and geography, barometric and thermometric observations, non-specific field trips and rambling travel diaries brought him, if not to a dead end, then certainly to a confusing crossroads where an amateur scientist alone could not have expected to select a program of investigation worthy of a professional.

Yet there did exist at that time in the viceroyalty a community of scientists, and a surprisingly vital one at that. The Botanical Expedition, begun in 1783, started work in Mariquita, but was ordered by the viceroy to return to Bogota in 1789 and had grown to become an exceedingly active scientific and cultural institution. José Celestino Mutis, educated as a physician and ordained as a priest, director of the expedition, was a world-class botanist. His correspondence with Linnaeus—father and son—and his relations with the Jardín Botánico de Madrid had established him as a prime investigator in tropical American botany.

Why did Caldas not establish contact with Mutis until 1801? Why did he not turn seriously to the study of plant life until his encounter with Humboldt and Bonpland? Why did he spend five years struggling as a solitary scientist? How did Caldas's lack of communication affect the rest of his career?

We can find answers to the first three questions by following the path which led the Granadian from astronomy to botany. As for the final question any response would necessarily be speculative, but we can begin to offer some probable consequences.

A CHOICE OF INSTRUMENTS

To encounter the reasons for Caldas's strange isolation we should take into account three components—the practical, the programmatic and the personal.

From the practical point of view, it should be noted that Caldas apparently had received little or no instruction in botany but had been given at least some notions of physics and astronomy. The books he had at hand either dealt principally with physical and geographical phenomena, or at least these were the aspects that caught his eye. During his trip to Bogotá in 1796 when he could have introduced himself to Mutis but did not, Caldas came back with the instruments—barometers and thermometers—that were to be found in the capital. And, although he recorded plant observations as early as 1795, he was thwarted in his desire to delve further into the subject by a lack of formal training and even appropriate references. Writing to Santiago Arroyo in 1795 he noted:

I would like to have a guide to the part [of my observations] that pertains to botany. . . . I am ignorant of the systems of Linnaeus and Tournefort; I can barely distinguish the parts of a plant. What I wish for most is to know their names and to be able to discern if they are known or if they are new.[1]

Furthermore, Caldas established a program based on measurements and instruments. He was meticulous in his attention to numerical values: temperature, barometric pressure, latitude, longitude, altitude, and he carefully computed average values—taking note of maxima and minima. He clearly enjoyed working with formulae, principally the conversion of barometric pressure to altitude, and making use of logarithms, the most complicated mathematics with which he was familiar. The construction, adaptation and maintenance of instruments also captured his attention during the period 1795–1799. While busy with the details of filling his barometer tubes or mounting his telescope, Caldas left himself little time for learning how to dry plants or to write descriptions.

Finally, mention must be made of the personal ingredient. Caldas seems to have been overly reserved with people he did not know. It is clear that he knew of Mutis and the Botanical Expedition even as a student of law in Bogotá from 1789 to 1792. The capital of the viceroyalty held no more than 20,000 to 30,000 inhabitants at the time. Surely Mutis, with his close relations to the viceroy, was among the notables of the city.

Later, in 1796, Caldas traveled to Bogotá with the express purpose of purchasing books and instruments for his scientific pursuits. It is incredible that he did not establish contact with the expedition at that point. The only explanation is that which Caldas wrote to Mutis in 1802, "I am irritated by my bashfulness for not having arrived at such a good father in 1796, when I could have, in Santa Fe [Bogotá]."[2]

An Anxious Apprentice

So it was that by 1799 Caldas had mastered the use of the barometer, thermometer, gnomon, quadrant and telescope. He had advanced as much as was possible with these instruments. Feeling the need to move

---

[1] Eduardo Posada, ed. *Cartas de Caldas*. Biblioteca de Historia Nacional. Volume 15. Imprenta Nacional. Bogotá. 1917, p. 5. Caldas refers here to the Swedish botanist Carl Linnaeus (b. 1707, d. 1778) and the French botanist Joseph Tournefort (b. 1656, d. 1708).

[2] Ibid., 195.

on to more substantive matters, and having no obvious alternatives in astronomy and geography, Caldas turned to botany. Writing to Arroyo he remarked, "How sorry am I for not having cultivated this study earlier."[3] And he intended to make up for lost time, "The truth is that since some time ago I have made botany my principal occupation—this in a virgin nation that offers a vast field where I can graze, be useful and enjoy myself."[4]

Yet enthused as he was, his progress was tempered by the lack of adequate reference material. His problem was even worse than that which he had encountered with the boiling point problem ("It is not in my books"). His problem was that he had no books. Or at least, very few. His friend and patron, Manuel Maria Arboleda, had purchased some books for him.[5] But, Caldas had no good listing of plant species nor was he able to obtain Linnaeus's *Filosofía Botánica*. He had insisted on this to his friends Arroyo and Pombo, but they had no luck finding the book in Bogotá.

Armed, then, with a few references and much enthusiasm, during 1800 and early 1801 Caldas tried to make headway on his own, organizing field trips with his friends in Popayán. They collected and categorized as best they could the plants they found in their outings.

In January 1801 Caldas decided to establish contact with Mutis, sending him three plants for proper identification. But at that point he interrupted his work on botany to prepare the article published in *Correo Curioso* (see Chapter I) and then devote himself entirely to the boiling point problem (see Chapter II). By August of 1801 he was preparing hurriedly for his trip to Quito to defend his family's interests in a lawsuit. Apparently the intensity of his commitment to botany was waning.

But as he was readying his departure, he received a letter from Mutis. Although the director of the Botanical Expedition was an active correspondent with a great number of persons throughout the viceroyalty, America and Europe, it was somewhat remarkable that he should write to Caldas since he had not written to Mutis. Caldas had sent the plants to Mutis via his friends in Bogotá and without an accompanying note. It was undoubtedly the friendly assistance of Santiago Arroyo, Miguel Pombo, Camilo Torres and Caldas's note in *Correo Curioso* that spurred the Spaniard's letter.

Accompanying the letter were "two good barometer tubes and the masterworks of Linnaeus."[6] Caldas was overjoyed. Finally an impediment to his studies had been removed. He wrote:

---

[3] Ibid., 30.
[4] Ibid., 31.
[5] Caldas names these titles and authors: *Flora*—Joseph Quer; *Parte Práctica*—Linnaeus; *Curso de Botánica*—Ortega and Palau.
[6] Eduardo Posada, ed. *Cartas de Caldas*. Biblioteca de Historia Nacional. Volume 15. Imprenta Nacional. Bogotá. 1917, p. 84.

[I have seen] this work [Linnaeus], the only of its kind, the basis of botany, the code within which are hidden the knowledge and laws of that science, yesterday, the third of August [1801] at nine o'clock at night—fortunate day and hour which will begin an epoch of my botanical studies.[7]

Because his trip to Quito could be delayed no longer, Caldas packed his copy of Linnaeus for the journey south and took care to begin a diary of botanical observations to be made along the way. Nevertheless, both his interest in botany and his correspondence with Mutis suffered an inevitable interruption while he settled in Quito and brushed up on his jurisprudence.[8]

When Caldas met with Humboldt in the beginning of 1802 they conversed mostly about astronomy and geography. Later, feeling a bit more confidant, Caldas explored Humboldt's knowledge of the boiling point problem. Thus, between 1799 when he announced his renewed interest in botany, and early 1802, Caldas's self-instruction was fragmented and haphazard.

He then had the good fortune of being invited to accompany Humboldt and Bonpland during their retreat to Chillo, the country estate of the Marques de Selvalegre. During February and March 1802, Caldas shared a room with Bonpland. Thirty-seven days of instruction, reading, copying, field trips, plant descriptions, skeletons and the like gave Caldas an intensive course in botany.

The role played by Bonpland in Caldas's formal encounter with botany cannot be overemphasized. The impression given by Caldas is that while Humboldt dealt with a great range of subjects—geology, botany, zoology, astronomy, anthropology and so forth—and while the baron displayed an incredible amount of energy in his study of the vast sweep of nature, it was Bonpland who pursued the study of plant life in a meticulous, ordered, detailed and persistent manner.

Although Humboldt maintained a certain reserve with respect to Caldas, (". . . he writes everything in German to make it more obscure"[9]), Bonpland took on the role of tutor with pleasure, "Bonpland, the sage and profound Bonpland, has lent me his books, his immense herbarium and his counsel; allowing me to take a place in his study and copy all that I want."[10]

Bonpland not only allowed the Granadian to study and copy manuscripts but organized an active course of study as well. Caldas described his apprenticeship, "I hope to make myself a botanist and have begun to write descriptions in Latin, to which one must become accustomed.

[7] Ibid., 82.
[8] The outcome of the litigation is a mystery. Caldas was certainly perturbed at having to take up the cause of his father versus that of his uncle. Somehow, though, the problem evaporated as he became more and more involved with the work of the Expedition.
[9] Eduardo Posada, ed. *Cartas de Caldas*. Biblioteca de Historia Nacional. Volume 15. Imprenta Nacional. Bogotá. 1917, p. 190.
[10] Ibid., 119.

He has made for me a plan of study and practice in botany."[11] He added, "I go out with this friendly and sage botanist to collect plants. I am building an excellent herbarium; he puts the names and has given me paper to dry the plants."[12]

During the month-long retreat Caldas also had his first chance to study the Flora Peruana which had been produced by the Botanical Expedition to Peru. He reported having made "continual inquiries"[13] of Bonpland on the matter. In addition, he managed to constitute his own herbarium consisting of two hundred specimens. Finally, upon his return to Quito, Caldas could write that:

[I have seen] . . . Bonpland describe plants and form herbaria. Now I have begun my own and it consists of more than two hundred dried plants, many now described. I have progressed a great deal with respect to descriptions—as I would simply write my own description, Bonpland would correct it with the plant in view. I have completed some, all in Latin, that Bonpland has approved.[14]

An Honorary Member

Just as Caldas's self-directed botanical apprenticeship suffered numerous detours, so did his entry into the Botanical Expedition. His first contact with Mutis was tentative, but clearly directed at establishing himself as a correspondent. When he finally received Mutis's first letter, Caldas responded with an unbridled adulation that was characteristic of his letters to his mentor:

What contrast is not to be found between the two of us. You are sage, known to all Europe, praised in the North by the son of Linnaeus, appreciated by the Nation, deserving the confidence of our august sovereign, director of a brilliant expedition whose precious fruits are impatiently awaited by the world of knowledge. I am ignorant, unknown to my own countrymen, living a dark and sometimes miserable life in a corner of America, without books, without instruments, without means of knowledge and unable to be of service to my country.[15]

But the arrival of Humboldt momentarily came between Caldas and the expedition. The prospect of accompanying the baron overshadowed everything else from January to April of 1802. Caldas hurried to urge his friends to enlist Mutis's support, not for his membership in the expedition, but as part of Humboldt's caravan. At that point Caldas also made his first contact with the merchant, José Ignacio de Pombo. A native of Popayán, Pombo had become a prominent and well-to-do member of the Consulado de Cartagena. He was uncle to Caldas's friend, Miguel Pombo.

---

11 Ibid., 131.
12 Ibid., 131.
13 Ibid., 128.
14 Ibid., 138.
15 Ibid., 55. In referring to "my country" Caldas means the Viceroyalty of Nueva Granada. Caldas showed great interest in the possible practical applications of his research for the economic development of the viceroyalty. He was proud to be a Granadian but did not mean to treat Nueva Granada as an entity separate from Spain.

Caldas looked to Pombo as a source of support for his travels with the Europeans.

Such was the tempest that grew from Humboldt's rejection of Caldas as a traveling companion that it took some time for the dust to settle. While Caldas was still seething, Mutis fortunately solved several problems at once by naming Caldas an honorary member of the Botanical Expedition in June 1802. This took the edge off the Humboldt-Caldas relationship. With Caldas no longer left high and dry by the baron, they soon became amiable correspondents until the Europeans left for Mexico in the following year.

Mutis managed to formalize relations with his most capable disciple in what was a case of being the right man, in the right place, at the right time. Certainly Caldas was the only man in Nueva Granada to have scaled volcanos with Humboldt, hunted for plants with Bonpland, copied the Europeans' notebooks, probed their knowledge and presented his own scientific labors for their judgment. And he was the only man to have merited written praise from Humboldt. This was a mark of approval that could not but have impressed Mutis.

Furthermore, Caldas was definitely in the right place. Mutis had traveled near Bogotá and Mariquita but never had reached the equator, yet this was also part of his mandate. He had little or no material from the region and no correspondent of any stature. Caldas was not only in Quito but also enthusiastic and well-trained. Mutis was in need of someone capable of collecting plant specimens with little guidance. Now he had his man.

Finally, that this was the right time is beyond doubt. Despite having a solid reputation as a botanist, the Spaniard had also gained fame as a chronic procrastinator. Whereas some of the findings of the Peruvian expedition were already available, in 1802 Mutis was still promising that his Flora de Bogotá would soon be complete. The delay in publishing had brought him close scrutiny by the viceroy, nagging insistence from the Spanish court and gleeful jeers from Hipolito Ruiz, director of the Peruvian expedition and Casimiro Ortega, director of the Jardín Botánico de Madrid and father-in-law to Ruiz. For Mutis there was much still to be done and little time left in which to do it. The Caldas that Mutis first became acquainted with through Arroyo, Torres and Pombo in 1801 must have been curiously enthusiastic and talented; but the Caldas who had been examined, trained and approved by Humboldt in 1802 was nothing less than a godsend.

As for Caldas, the position with the expedition put him back on his feet and headed in the right direction. He managed to recover from his disillusionment by directing his enthusiasm to the new challenge. The only sore point in the process was the "honorary" nature of his position. He had been named directly by Mutis and, as such, had no official status nor a secure salary. Although Mutis cared for Caldas's financial needs and often promised to arrange for an official appointment, the difficulty remained unresolved and caused more than a little discomfort for Caldas.

A Research Program

When Caldas became an honorary member of the Botanical Expedition in June 1802 he had already presented to Mutis a research program to be followed. His first discussions of a plan of work were written as part of his attempt to convince Mutis to support his proposed travel with Humboldt. Immediately following Humboldt's rejection Caldas amplified his proposal, this time as part of a one-man journey throughout equatorial America.[16] Mutis calmly counseled his pupil, slowly reducing the scope of the journey to, in, and around the Presidency of Quito.

Nevertheless, the main points of Caldas's program remained unchanged. For the next three years Mutis could only loosely guide Caldas's efforts and it is of interest to review what Caldas proposed as a benchmark for understanding what he later did or did not accomplish.

Caldas had a rather extensive list of projects to carry out. Yet every aspect of his research program dealt in some way with the world he ordinarily observed as he traveled throughout the viceroyalty. For economy's sake, the objects of Caldas's curiosity can be grouped as follows:

1. Botany
2. Hypsometry
3. Meteorology
4. Astronomy
5. The French Expedition
6. Maps

Following his apprenticeship with Bonpland, Caldas had gained confidence in his ability to search for, identify and collect plants. He had become familiar with the works of Linnaeus and to some extent the Flora de Peru, and had copied extensively from Bonpland's manuscripts and herbarium. He was careful to emphasize the possibility of bringing new plant collections to Mutis, certainly to insure his mentor's interest in allowing him to travel freely about the Presidency of Quito.

At this point Caldas began to define his ideas for a study of plant geography. The general notion of establishing maps of distributions versus altitude was to be applied not only to plants, but to animals and minerals as well. He was also interested in meeting Juan Tafalla who was continuing the work of the Peruvian expedition. Well aware of Mutis's dispute with the Peruvian expedition's botanists, Caldas made it clear that he was interested in learning what they knew only to work better in defense of Mutis's reputation.

Notwithstanding Caldas's growth as a botanist, his enthusiasm and his expectations that Mutis would tutor him ". . . as a father who trains a son,"[17] he still lacked the experience to carry out his assignments with the polish of a formally educated investigator. Thus he took an all-encompassing approach with regard to his work:

16 "Memoria sobre el plan de un viaje proyectado de Quito a la America septentrional" in *Obras Completas de Francisco José de Caldas*. Universidad Nacional de Colombia. Imprenta Nacional. Bogotá. 1966.

17 Eduardo Posada, ed. *Cartas de Caldas*. Biblioteca de Historia Nacional. Volume 15. Imprenta Nacional. Bogotá. 1917, p. 178.

Every plant that I encounter is either known to me or not. In the first case I will not delay in a long description of its fructification, and I will only describe its flowers, stems, leaves, roots, etc. If it is unknown to me I will procure to find it among the few books that I possess; if I find it there I proceed as in the first case; but if it is unknown to me and I do not find it in my books, I will make an ample description of all its parts. In all cases I will note where it grows and, as the altitudes of the places are known to me from my barometric measurements, I can add the zone that it inhabits, as I wrote to you in my first plan. I will add its common name, that given in the Indian tongue and finally I conclude with its medical virtues and its uses in the arts.[18]

Finally it is worth noting that in his numerous proposals to Mutis, Caldas does not discuss the problem of the cinchona tree. That he should omit reference to the most pressing issue for his mentor is an indication of the incompleteness of his training.

The boiling point problem still was of some interest. Caldas felt that he had found the unique solution even though he was not the first one to recognize the phenomenon. He planned to continue his measurements, making special emphasis on the need for observations at sea level, in order to compute more accurately the proportionality constant used in his formula.

Mutis offered to send Caldas's boiling point memoir to the new director of the Jardín Botánico de Madrid, Antonio Cavanilles (who replaced Casimiro Ortega). But Caldas asked him to delay saying, ". . . until I have finished my operations in Quito and Guayaquil . . . I believe that in six to eight months I can put in your hands all the material, and all the memoir, so that you might correct it, and put it in condition to see the light of day."[19]

As had become his custom since his travels near Popayán, Caldas planned to make regular measurements with his barometers and thermometers. He announced to Mutis that he would keep a diary of meteorological observations, a practice he later continued in the Observatory in Bogotá. He and Baron von Humboldt had made many measurements together in Quito. That gave Caldas the opportunity to improve his method of observation and to learn new formulae for computing altitudes.

With regard to astronomy, Caldas owed a great deal to Humboldt. The Prussian had taught him how to use an octant and to understand tables of atmospheric refraction[20] at different altitudes. He had further provided Caldas with a star catalog, an ephemerides, an octant and sold him his own quadrant. Caldas noted, "He has put me in condition to direct myself and to do something useful."[21]

[18] Ibid., 179.

[19] Ibid., 180.

[20] Atmospheric refraction is the difference between the true position and the observed position of a heavenly body caused by the presence of the atmosphere in the line of sight between object and observer. The amount of refraction lessens as one climbs to higher altitudes since the observer rises above part of the atmosphere. This was a subject which was quite appropriate for investigation by Caldas.

[21] *Obras Completas de Francisco José de Caldas.* Universidad Nacional de Colombia. Imprenta Nacional. Bogotá. 1966, p. 300.

Accordingly, Caldas asked Mutis to provide him with a chronometer, telescope, copy of Astronomia by Lalande and a nautical almanac. He planned to pursue three projects:

1. Measurement of longitudes for the purpose of map-making. Caldas expected to use the observations of solar eclipses, lunar eclipses and the occultations of the moons of Jupiter.
2. Atmospheric refraction. Caldas hoped to compare his measurements with those made by Bouger during the French Expedition.
3. A map of the southern sky.

The French expedition that had traveled to the equator to determine the shape of the Earth continued to cast a spell over Caldas. Confronted with the possibility of enjoying patronage for travel near the equator, he suggested to Mutis that he visit nearby monuments, perhaps those of the Incans and other Indian tribes. His real interest, however, was to visit the region in which the European scientists had labored. He made many suggestions on this point: reconstruction of the pyramids that marked the extremes of the 1° arc; repeating the measurement of the equatorial degree; correction of possible measurements in earlier measurements of longitude. Although Mutis may have lent a sympathetic ear, this project was primarily of interest to Caldas.

Finally, Caldas suggested making a map of the Presidency of Quito. This was to be a prelude to a political map of the viceroyalty (which he apparently never made). He was pleased to note that his meticulousness was in contrast to that of Humboldt who ". . . mixes the certain with the doubtful."[22] As with retracing the path of the French Expedition, map-making was a project that interested mainly Caldas.

With a long list of projects, an honorary membership in the Botanical Expedition, a passport that Mutis had obtained from the viceroy, some instruments, books and notes, Francisco José de Caldas looked forward to his encounter with nature near the Equator. As a scientist, at last he had found a community.

---

22 Ibid., 309.

V. WORKING FOR THE EXPEDITION

Once it became clear to Mutis that he would have a new member of the expedition, he turned quickly to the problem of financial support. Mutis at seventy years of age had become, if not rich, then certainly accommodated. He was a priest, physician, professor and "primer botánico" in the viceroyalty of Nueva Granada. In addition, he had obtained control, for a time, of the commerce of cinchona bark. Thus he enjoyed enough economic flexibility to provide part of Caldas's support from his own resources.

Mutis knew that it would not be enough. So he followed Caldas's lead and looked to the Cartagenan businessman, Pombo. The two men already had a well-established friendship. Pombo and Mutis had been correspondents at least since 1788. From the inception of the Botanical Expedition Pombo had been an enthusiastic supporter. He acted as a kind of one-man communication center, keeping Mutis advised on news of the court and the comings and goings of merchant vessels from Spain. He was an active member of the Consulado de Cartagena, a body designated to promote economic development within the viceroyalty. Furthermore, he managed the shipments of cinchona bark Mutis sent to Spain.

Pombo was well informed of Caldas's activities. Certainly Pombo's nephew, Miguel—a friend of Caldas, must have made some comment to his uncle regarding the many and varied projects of his friend. And he had already been contacted when Caldas sought to accompany Humboldt.

Yet the most convincing evidence for the elder Pombo for spending his own funds on the novice botanist must have been the opinions of Humboldt. Pombo wrote to Mutis, "The Baron speaks of him [Caldas] with praise and admires the progress he has made with the strength of his wits, without support, means, books or instruments in the most sublime arts of the natural and exact sciences."[1]

Pombo was generous in his support of Caldas, sending him money, books, maps and other materials as he could. He even conceded to fund one of Caldas's younger brothers as an assistant. Such was the merchant's enthusiasm that he suggested to Mutis the organization of a study trip to Europe for Caldas, his nephew Miguel, and Mutis's nephew, Sinforoso.

The relations between benefactor and beneficiary got off to a good start with each stressing to Mutis the merits of the other. Pombo wrote

---

[1] Guillermo Hernandez de Alba, ed. *Archivo Epistolar Del Sabio Naturalista Don José Celestino Mutis.* Volume IV. Instituto Colombiano de Cultura Hispánica. Bogotá. 1983, p. 100.

of Caldas, "His correctness, his love of his fellows and the sciences, his moderation and purity of habit, his patriotism, his zeal and tireless application, his good judgement and, finally, his piety at an early age, do make him an extraordinary man."[2]

Caldas was equally eager to praise, "That generous citizen, Pombo, has wanted to share with you the glory of protecting this expedition; he has written me letters which will eternally honor him and has facilitated many useful channels."[3]

Not the least of those "useful channels" was the Marques de Selvalegre, Juan Pio Montufar, host to Humboldt and Bonpland in Quito and father of Carlos Montufar, the "irresolute youth" who accompanied the Europeans and took what Caldas felt was his own rightful position. Montufar was a friend and associate of Pombo. Despite his irritation with Montufar's son, Caldas managed to accommodate himself to the circumstances. Just as he could demonstrate a deep and seemingly unalterable animosity, so could he rapidly swing to limitless praise when the need arose. Thus, in spite of the grudge he held against the younger Montufar, Caldas easily wrote the following in 1804:

The Marques de Selvalegre, owner of this land rich in herds [of sheep] has given me a good recommendation so that I might receive all possible service from his overseer. This is not the only occasion in which we have named in our travels this generous and magnificent "Quiteño," and it will not be the last; many are the services received from his hand.[4]

Caldas in mid-1802 was eager to get to work. Praised by Humboldt, funded by Pombo and guided by Mutis he faced the challenge of exploring the Ecuadorean Andes as a solitary representative of the Botanical Expedition pitted against an immense world of lush vegetation.

Though Mutis had tacitly approved Caldas's entire program of investigation, in time Caldas increasingly emphasized studies of botany and geography. His work on the boiling point problem suffered from a simple problem—lack of thermometers. Common to his letters to Pombo and Mutis were requests that he be sent new thermometers with all due speed. Both men complied. On at least one occasion though, the thermometer arrived in pieces and Caldas complained that he would be unable to continue his studies.

Caldas persisted and he later received usable instruments. He was able to report that the boiling point temperature depends on the motion of the air above the water. When the air was fanned, the boiling point would occur at a lower point than when the air remained static. Beyond this observation he made little progress. Caldas had anticipated further rectification of his proportionality constant and measurement of sea-level

2 Ibid., 106.

3 Eduardo Posada, ed. *Cartas de Caldas*. Biblioteca de Historia Nacional. Volume 15. Imprenta Nacional. Bogotá. 1917, p. 196.

4 *Obras Completas de Franciso José de Caldas*. Universidad Nacional de Colombia. Imprenta Nacional. Bogotá. 1966, p. 444.

values of air pressure and boiling point temperature. Perhaps the rigors of his travels or the pressure he felt regarding the cinchona problem interfered with his work on hypsometry. In early 1804, he included the boiling point problem in a revised program to Mutis, but at that point he seems to have encountered a dead end and never did produce the "finished" memoir he had earlier promised to Mutis.

In astronomy Caldas suffered a similar fate. Though Mutis provided him with a telescope and chronometer, his work on astronomy was limited to measurements of latitude. He did observe the Transit of Mercury (see Chapter III), an occasional lunar eclipse and endured the torment of cloudy skies for a solar eclipse in February 1803. And he did refer to the existence of a diary of astronomical observations (which apparently was later lost). The interest he had taken in the problem of atmospheric refraction (probably as a result of his conversations with Humboldt) was thwarted by the lack of a trained co-observer.

But Caldas was unable to organize a program of original work in astronomy. So he contented himself with the pleasures of observing, took what notes he could and hoped that he might learn something from his raw data upon his return to Bogotá.

SCALING THE ANDES

Not only did Caldas have a well-formulated plan of study; he also enjoyed little interference from Mutis with its execution. Thus he chose to leave Quito in July 1802 for a field trip to the towns of Ibarra and Otavalo, returning to Quito in December.

The trip was all-encompassing as with his earlier travels between Popayán and Bogotá. Caldas never missed an opportunity to take measurements with his barometer, to note new plants or comment on plant geography. During his excursion to Ibarra and Otavalo he visited an Incan monument and sent a plan of it to Mutis. He took samples of plants used for dyes and began a collection of bird specimens and descriptions.

The highlight of the trip was Caldas's scaling of the volcano at Imbabura, of which he wrote a vivid description. Caldas was a veteran of volcano climbing. He had earlier scaled the Puracé Volcano near Popayán and the Pichincha Volcano near Quito.

He customarily traveled with Indian guides and mules to carry his instruments and provisions. The caravan would travel by day and stay in the homes of mountain dwelling Indians by night. Caldas described their situation:

And who could believe that some thirty leagues from Quito would be found a family nearly in the same state as during the epoch of the "conquista"? I only make note of the surprise that they felt when shown our instruments; they are unable to distinguish a spoon from a thermometer, and thought that all we carried had to do with cooking or our wardrobe.[5]

---

[5] Ibid., 447.

At the first hint of dawn Caldas was afoot to make good use of the day-light and guard against the freezing temperatures they would reach at the summit. He continued:

The path was covered with sleet and this made the climb more terrible for the way was unsure and most of all because of the cold, which increased every moment, had numbed my feet. I keenly wished to see this unknown crater, and I scorned all dangers. From precipice to precipice we arrived at nine o'clock in the morning at the crater's border, covered with sweat and fatigue. What a spectacle! My soul was filled with horror and a secret pleasure. I did not tire of observing and admiring this frightful nature. The burned and broken openings, edges, pumice, sand, sulfur, snow, mud, precipices and confusion were the objects present before my eyes.[6]

Caldas in some ways gives the impression of a timid and not particularly robust person, but certainly there were moments, especially those associated with making an observation, when fear and weakness were of no consequence. This was such an occasion. Caldas decided to descend to the floor of the crater to measure its altitude barometrically:

I was afraid, but the ease with which my guide had passed gave me comfort and I confronted the danger. I had taken only three steps on the pumice when all began to move and, unable to maintain myself afoot, I sat down, and even in this situation I began to slide toward the bottom of the terrible crater; I thought my life's end had come and I gave a call to my guide. This generous Indian turned toward me with extraordinary courage, threw himself to the same danger in which he saw me, grabbed my right arm, pulled me from the precipice and gave me life.[7]

THE ROAD TO MALBUCHO

The dangers and discomforts of his science were made manifest to Caldas not only at the heights of the Andean peaks. The depths of the tropical rain forest also challenged him.

While waiting for instructions from Mutis, Caldas took time to introduce himself to the president of Quito, Baron Carondelet, surely with the purpose of requesting Carondelet's sponsorship for his activities. At the time there was interest in opening a trafficable route between Quito and the Pacific coast. Caldas convinced the president that an earlier plan was based on faulty geographical measurements. Carondelet commissioned Caldas to produce a new plan. Although Caldas mentioned that Carondelet had $40,000 pesos available for the project, it appears most likely that he used funds sent by Mutis and Pombo to cover his expenses.

There were a number of factors which motivated Caldas to accept the commission. First, Mutis had sent his disciple a passport from the viceroy in May 1803 and ordered the collection of flora near Quito. Furthermore,

6 Eduardo Posada, ed. *Cartas de Caldas*. Biblioteca de Historia Nacional. Volume 15. Imprenta Nacional. Bogotá. 1917, p. 186.
7 Ibid., 188.

Caldas wished to meet with Juan Tafalla who was continuing the work of the Peruvian expedition and was located in the vicinity of Malbucho, along the planned route. Finally, Mutis had begun to impress upon Caldas the importance of the cinchona problem. Caldas considered that the trip would give him an opportunity to do some work on the matter.

The trip began in mid-July 1803 and lasted until the beginning of October. The primary points of interest were a map of the route and the collection of plant specimens. As he moved farther along Caldas found it increasingly difficult to work. His topographic observations were made by rope because, he said, ". . . the geometric methods are impracticable in these places covered with forest as old as the world."[8]

During the twelve days he spent near the town of Malbucho conditions were harsh for all types of work, he complained, "Every night and every afternoon it rained without interruption; everything decomposes and nothing can resist a climate so contrary to the health of man and the progress of the sciences."[9]

Caldas met with Tafalla for his first in-depth contact with the collections described in the *Flora de Peru*. Caldas then stayed alone several days waiting for provisions and funds sent by Pombo and brought by Caldas's younger brother. His intention was to avoid the extra return trip and devote more time to collecting plants.

What he got was a serious and persistent case of malaria. Caldas reported on his travels to Mutis in a letter that he had to dictate for lack of strength to write with his own hand, "I left on the 14th of July to enter these forests where I have stayed until the 3rd of October, when I arrived to this village [Ibarra] with my health quite undone, after a continuous chain of fatigues, labors and, I must say, misery."[10]

As for the results of his excursion, the botanical side was negative. Caldas found no cinchona trees and remarked that they ". . . exist only in the imagination of the Quiteños."[11] Even more seriously he once again had to face the consequences of his isolation and lack of formal training. Of his meeting with Tafalla, he commented:

I became truly despondent upon seeing that I had lost two-thirds of my labor for the lack of this opus [Flora del Peru] absolutely necessary for a botanist in America. If I would have had that I would not have wasted my time and health writing and drawing known and published plants, and would have satisfied myself with skeletons to complete the collection.[12]

On the other hand, Caldas did produce a map of the route which he presented to Carondelet (see Map 4). He also sent a copy to Mutis with the wish that it be forwarded to the director of the Jardín Botánico de

---

[8] Ibid., 216.
[9] Ibid., 216.
[10] Ibid., 215.
[11] Ibid., 215.
[12] Ibid., 218.

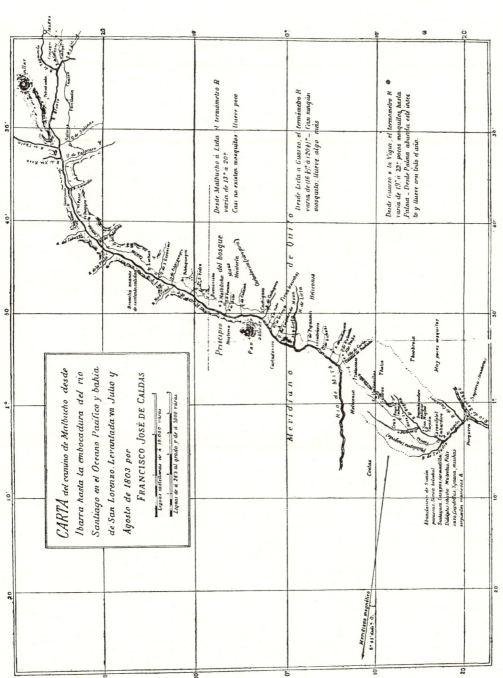

MAP 4. Caldas's Map of the Route through Malbucho. Reprinted from Federico Gonzalez Suarez. *Un Opúsculo de Caldas: Páginas de Historia Colombiana. Academia Colombiana de Historia. ABC. Bogotá. 1944.*

Madrid, Antonio Cavanilles, and would serve as evidence in favor of a permanent position with the expedition.

It is worth noting, with reference to the map, of Caldas's interest in measurement. He included not only latitudes and longitudes, but also the magnetic field directions and temperature variations for different zones. He further pointed out the abundance of certain plants, the beginning of the rain forest and, understandably, the presence or absence of mosquitoes.

FOLLOWING THE FRENCH EXPEDITION

Among the first books on science that Caldas read were those that he acquired in Bogotá in 1795, written by the members of the French Expedition to the Equator. Throughout his correspondence Caldas made reference to Bouger and La Condamine. Their labors in the determination of the length of a degree of arc at the Equator were truly inspirational for the Granadian. They established for him the travel, observation and measurement style for the study of the natural world.

Caldas held Bouger and La Condamine in the highest esteem and wrote:

If there has ever been a traveller who deserves credence it is without a doubt La Condamine and his illustrious companion, Bouger. How different from Ulloa! [The Spanish official who accompanied the French scientists]. This Spaniard, young, naive, without experience, believed what he was told and, anxious to tell Europe new things and make his travels of interest, has gathered all that he found curious and rare. From that may come many fables and exaggeration presented as half-truths. Humboldt has just visited us. We have only seen two of his letters in number 18 of the Anales de Ciencias Naturales and we can declare that in more than one place he has erred.[13]

Caldas pestered Mutis on the subject of the French expedition. He suggested rebuilding the pyramids that marked the baseline, and making a new measurement of the degree of arc. But Mutis apparently paid no attention. He had other problems at hand.

In late 1804, on the road to study the cinchona tree in the province of Loja, Caldas took the opportunity to make a detour and follow La Condamine's route through the area north of Quito. He visited the town of Cuenca where a church tower served as a reference point for the work of Godin and Jorge Juan (see Chapter I).

Near Cuenca he visited the Yarqui plain where the European scientists had worked. There he came upon a marble marker they had left, but in an unexpected situation. Caldas wrote a colorful account:

Everyone knows that the [French] academics finished their labors of the measurement of the degree near the equator in the Tarqui plain; that they measured a second baseline similar to that in Yarqui; and that in one of the nearby "haci-

---

[13] Obras Completas de Franciso José de Caldas. Universidad Nacional de Colombia. Imprenta Nacional. Bogotá. 1966, p. 470.

endas" they established their southern observatory. At that time this [the "hacienda"] belonged to a resident of Cuenca named don M. Sempertegui. Here, M. de La Condamine left a marble tablet. . . . But the new owners who replaced Sempertegui took it from its place and gave it a destiny different from that which it had originally. Instead of honoring the memory and results of observations which decided the figure of the Earth . . . it was used as a bridge over a ditch, covered with dirt and buried. What destiny! Is there perhaps some enemy of the celebrated journey? Everything is lost, ruined by barbarians.[14]

Confronted with an insult to the memory of his cherished expedition, Caldas quickly decided how to remedy the degradation of the tablet. He stole it.

The marble tablet was carried by Caldas's pack animals the length of the Andes from southern Ecuador to Bogotá. It was not until after Caldas's death, the liberation of the Spanish American colonies and the atomization of Nueva Granada that the Colombian government returned the tablet to Ecuador.

PLANT GEOGRAPHY

Notwithstanding the dangers and the "misery" of his travels, it seems fair to say that Caldas had found peace in the idyllic routes amid natural wonders in tropical America. He enjoyed the freedom to measure and observe, to write and draw, to speculate and analyze all that surrounded him. He was far from the growing turmoil in Europe but enjoyed the protection and support of the Botanical Expedition, an institution created by the Spanish monarchy.

Certainly, though, it is fair to ask—what were the results of his efforts? Did any substantive scientific advances arise from Caldas's lonely crusade in the Andes? The answer is affirmative for it was during his travels in Ecuador that Caldas clarified his ideas about the geographical distribution of plant life: for every plant species a set of limits could be observed that would define a habitable zone. These limits—maxima and minima of altitude and latitude—could be compiled, and maps, or distribution profiles, could be drawn to show how plants were located throughout any terrain.

Caldas felt that the concept of plant geography (or phytogeography) was his most important intellectual effort. Yet he was not able to develop it fully. Had he joined the Botanical Expedition in 1796, or become a disciple of Mutis at that time, his journeys near the Equator would have served for the gathering of data to polish his ideas. Had his life been spared during the Spanish reconquest of 1814–1816, phytogeography would have been the principal line of research for the rest of his life. As it was, his work on the subject was limited to some tentative observations about cultivated plants, detailed measurements of the cinchona tree, commentaries and notes that were never organized.

---

[14] Ibid., 495.

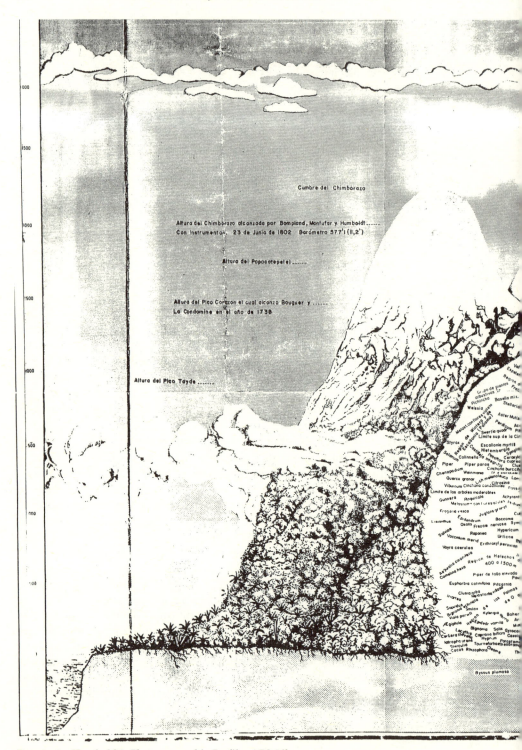

FIGURE 6.   Humboldt's Phytogeographic Profile, APS Library

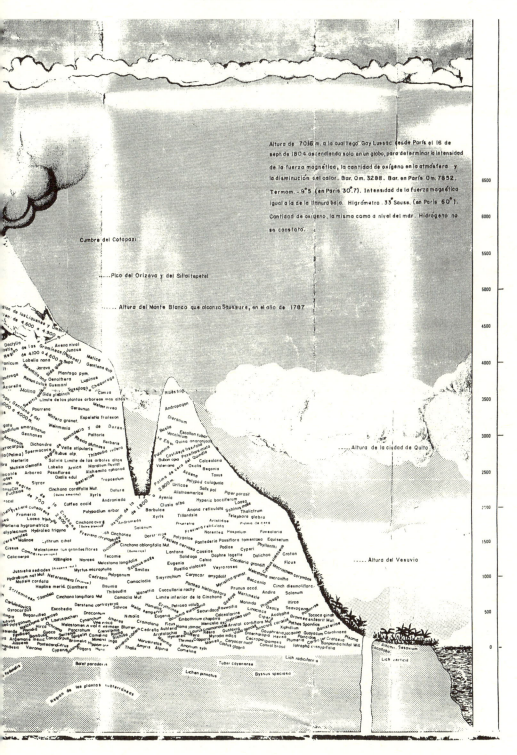

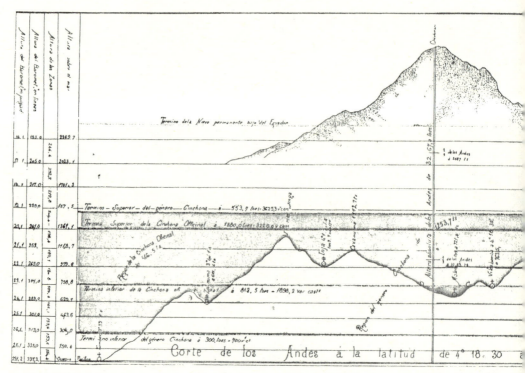

FIGURE 7.   Caldas's Phytogeographic Profile. Reprinted from Federico Gonzalez Suarez. *Un Opúsculo*

The subject of phytogeography was of interest not only to Caldas, but also to Humboldt. Indeed it has been suggested[15] that he rejected Caldas's company and hurriedly published his own results upon his return to Europe to preempt any possible priority dispute brought by the Granadian. Furthermore, some Colombian writers have insinuated that Humboldt was guilty of plagiarism. A careful look at the record will give each man his due.

Before his arrival in America, Humboldt had traveled extensively in Europe. His observations of the natural world along a varied topography had brought him face to face with the possibility of a plant geography. He remarked, "Since my youth I have accumulated ideas for an opus of this nature."[16]

Humboldt's observations of American flora began with his arrival at Venezuela. He, like Caldas, maintained a diary of observations and carried a barometer at all times. In Bogota, Caldas's friend Arroyo saw the baron's maps of altitude distributions, procured a copy and sent it

[15] Armando Espinosa. "Relaciones entre Caldas y Humboldt" in Estado Actual de la Investigación sobre Caldas. Universidad del Cauca. Popayán. 1986.

[16] Alexander von Humboldt. *Ideas para una Geografía de las Plantas mas un Cuadro de la Naturaleza de los Países Tropicales.* Jardín Botánico 'José Celestino Mutis.' Bogotá. 1985, p. i.

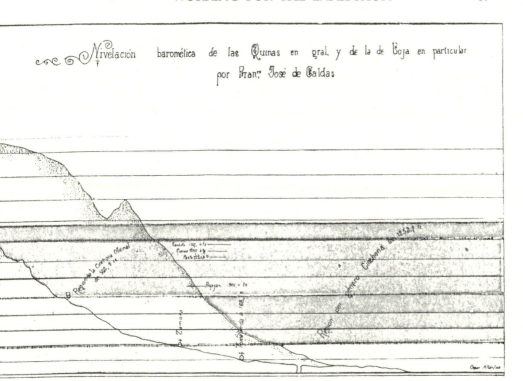

Nivelación barométrica de las Quinas en gral. y de la de Loja en particular por Franc. José de Caldas

de Caldas: Paginas de Historia Colombiana. **Academia Colombiana de Historia. ABC. Bogotá. 1944.**

to Caldas. The description given by Caldas is a ". . . profile of barometric measurements from Cartagena to Santa Fe [Bogotá] with latitudes, altitudes, minerals and other curiosities. . . ."[17]

Caldas's letters do not mention plant geography prior to his learning of Humboldt's efforts. He did not even have a reliable taxonomic reference until August 1801. Furthermore, he began his first diary of exclusively botanical observations on the road from Popayán to Quito after receiving the book of Linnaeus from Mutis, and Humboldt's profile from Arroyo.

Clearly, when the two men met in Quito it was Humboldt who had a program for developing the concept of phytogeography. However, Caldas should not be unduly slighted. He knew the geography of Nueva Granada from Bogotá to Quito better than any of his contemporaries. His diaries and copious measurements of altitude, latitude and temperature had provided him with the seed of an idea—that geographical limits could be established to the habitats of plants. Though he lacked the formal training necessary to crystallize his idea, he was headed in that direction before Humboldt's arrival and should in no way be charged with having appropriated the baron's initiative.

---

[17] Eduardo Posada, ed. *Cartas de Caldas*. Biblioteca de Historia Nacional. Volume 15. Imprenta Nacional. Bogotá. 1917, p. 100.

Indeed, it must be recalled that Humboldt found much of Caldas's work worthy of taking note—his map of Timaná, his hypsometric measurements and his astronomical observations. Caldas also had numerous barometric measurements of locations along the Andes that Humboldt had no occasion to make. It is not unlikely that these measurements were useful to Humboldt.

Before leaving the South American mainland from the port of Guayaquil in February 1803, Humboldt produced a manuscript entitled "Ideas for a Geography of Plants with a Nature Map of the Tropics based on Observations and Measurements made between the parallels 10° N and 10° S during the years 1799, 1800, 1801, 1802 and 1803."[18]

Humboldt dedicated the manuscript to Mutis and sent it to the Marques de Selvalegre with the request that it be forwarded to the director of the Botanical Expedition. The marques gave the manuscript to Caldas who held it for fifteen days in order to make a copy for himself. When he sent it along to Mutis he included a manuscript of his own, "Memoir on the Distribution of Plants that are Cultivated near the Equator" (a translation of this memoir is presented in Appendix B)—which dealt primarily with the altitude at which wheat could be cultivated, along with notes on other grains and vegetables.[19]

Humboldt's manuscript and altitude profile (see Fig. 6) demonstrate his voracious appetite for data. He plotted a number of variables versus altitude: atmospheric refraction, visibility, comparative altitudes, electric phenomena, cultivated plants, decrease in gravity, color of the sky, humidity, atmospheric pressure, atmospheric temperature, chemistry of the atmosphere, snow line, animal species, boiling point temperature. Such wide-ranging commentary was beyond Caldas's reach.

The baron was quick to publish his manuscript when he arrived in Europe. A French version appeared in 1805 and a German version in 1807. Caldas himself published a version of the work in 1809 in his *Semanario* (see Chapter VIII). He accompanied it with a preface and notes, and was explicit in giving Humboldt ample credit, "We have followed the steps of this illustrious traveller with the same objectives, and with the 'Plant Geography' in our hands. . . ."[20]

Caldas announced the publication of a similar work of his own, "Fitogeografia del Ecuador." This was never completed. Upon his return to Bogotá he was assigned to direct the Astronomical Observatory and his plant collections were turned over to Mutis. Following Mutis's death in 1808 and the events surrounding the revolution all activity regarding the expedition slowed down. When Caldas pleaded for clemency with his

[18] Alexander von Humboldt. *Ideas para una Geografía de las Plantas mas un Cuadro de la Naturaleza de los Países Tropicales.* Jardín Botánico 'José Celestino Mutis.' Bogotá. 1985.

[19] *Obras Completas de Francisco José de Caldas.* Universidad Nacional de Colombia. Imprenta Nacional. Bogotá. 1966, p. 335.

[20] Alexander von Humboldt. *Ideas para una Geografía de las Plantas mas un Cuadro de la Naturaleza de los Países Tropicales.* Jardín Botánico 'José Celestino Mutis.' Bogotá. 1985, p. XIX.

executioners he named the "Fitogeografia" as the most important of his works left unfinished (see Fig. 7).

Could it be that Humboldt regarded Caldas as a rival? I believe that for Humboldt the concept of phytogeography was especially important. He found in Nueva Granada two men, Mutis and Caldas, capable of developing the idea, and one, Caldas, already with the raw data available to do it. While there was no doubt about to Humboldt's priorities on the matter, he found it in his interest to expedite publication.

VI. THE QUININE QUANDARY

While Caldas was riding blissfully amidst the natural wonders of the equatorial Andes, accompanied by his Indian guides, his instruments, his notebooks and his plant collections, both of his patrons, Mutis and Pombo, were beginning to have second thoughts about their beneficiary's investigations.

The breaking point came near the end of 1803 when Caldas asked Mutis to send two painters to aid in the work of illustrating the plants in his collection—a reasonable request, especially since Mutis had recently assigned two painters to his nephew Sinforoso. The problem was not the request for two assistants, but rather the feeling that Caldas was out of control. Neither Pombo nor Mutis could predict where Caldas's research program would lead, how long it would take to complete, how much it would cost or what benefits would be brought to the Botanical Expedition. Furthermore, Caldas was not the obedient disciple he seemed at first. He was confidently following his own instincts and interests even if it meant ignoring to some degree the instructions he had received.

Pombo was the first to react. Mutis apparently acceded in letting Pombo deal with Caldas in a strict and direct manner. In a letter to Mutis, Pombo complained of Caldas's spreading himself too thin and of the delays associated with the trip to Malbucho. He continued by spelling out to Mutis his thoughts on the matter:

In these circumstances it seems to me that not only should he [Caldas] be denied the painters and other items he requests, but also should be warned that if he does not proceed immediately to Guayaquil and from there continue without delay to Chocó [Pacific coastal region of Colombia] to complete the objectives he proposed you will be obliged to suspend your support, to use those funds in other items more appropriate and useful to the Expedition.[1]

Not the least of Pombo's worries were the limits of his own philanthropy. He said, "I will also tell him . . . that having to attend children and other obligations I cannot . . . support him further, especially as he is not following his proposed trip . . . and when he initially only asked $1000 pesos for a voyage to Lima, Mexico, Habana and Cartagena."[2]

In November 1803 Pombo wrote to Caldas ordering him to proceed to Chocó or face the termination of Pombo's support. Furthermore, Pombo

---

[1] Guillermo Hernandez de Alba, ed. *Archivo Epistolar Del Sabio Naturalista Don José Celestino Mutis*. Four Volumes. Instituto Colombiano de Cultura Hispánica. Bogotá. 1983. Volume IV, p. 119.

[2] Ibid., 120.

accused Caldas of remaining in Quito instead of working in the country-side; of working on useless interminable and costly projects; and of having spent three times what he needed. Mutis, who had been ill, finally made it known to Caldas that he was expected to return soon to Bogotá, but he again lapsed into silence until mid-1804.

The discontent in Cartagena and Bogotá caught Caldas by surprise. He was hurt by the criticism and somewhat unnerved. He quickly sent Mutis a box of plant skeletons, drawings and descriptions as well as a collection of bird skeletons. This was the first such shipment Caldas had made to his mentor.

In his defense Caldas tried to clarify many points. He presented a pain-fully detailed expense account to counter Pombo's assertion that he was a spendthrift. He recalled that it was Mutis who had ordered him to stay in Quito. He complained that he was still suffering the ill effects of his journey to Malbucho and that no one expressed sympathy or gratitude for his efforts. But he did respond to the charges of overextending himself and announced, "I have pushed aside my inclinations and left nearly all for botany."[3]

The worried tone of Caldas's reply, the lameness of his own defense seems to have convinced Pombo who wrote to Mutis in April 1804, "Our friend Caldas has sent me a rather diffuse letter in which he specifies his labors, expenses, etc. to demonstrate that they were not useless as I had told him."[4]

THE CINCHONA PROBLEM

Although Mutis may have been concerned about the usefulness and cost of Caldas's investigations, there was a more pressing problem for the director of the Botanical Expedition. This was the issue of the efficacy of the bark of the cinchona tree as an anti-malarial remedy. The cinchona problem had arisen a century before Mutis's birth, plagued him throughout his career and outlasted both his efforts and those of a prodded disciple, Caldas, to find a solution.

Among the discoveries brought back to Spain by the "conquistadores" was the use of the bark of the cinchona tree—dried, ground and taken orally—as a specific remedy in the treatment of malaria. The bark con-tains the alkaloid, quinine, and its introduction "marked the first suc-cessful use of a chemical compound in combating infectious disease."[5]

Quinine became part of European medicine in the first half of the sev-enteenth century, almost certainly having been discovered first by South

3 Eduardo Posada, ed. *Cartas de Caldas*. Biblioteca de Historia Nacional. Volume 15. Imprenta Nacional. Bogotá. 1917.

4 Guillermo Hernandez de Alba, ed. *Archivo Epistolar Del Sabio Naturalista Don José Celestino Mutis*. Four Volumes. Instituto Colombiano de Cultura Hispánica. Bogotá. 1983. Volume IV, p. 124.

5 *Encyclopedia Britannica*. Volume 18, p. 968.

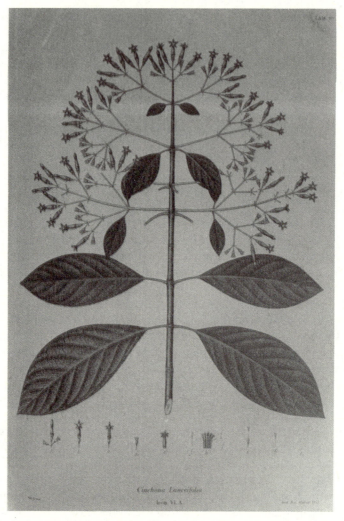

FIGURE 8. Cinchona Officinalis. Reprinted from Gabriel Fonnegra, ed. *Mutis y La Expedición Botánica (Documentos)*. El Ancora Editores. Bogotá. 1983.

American Indians. Curiously, the cinchona tree appeared to be highly localized in the province of Loja in the southern part of the Presidency of Quito.

The cinchona genus contains many species most of which are not effective anti-malarial agents. And therein lay the source of great difficulties for Mutis, a "fatal flaw" which shaped the destiny of this botanist, physician and priest.

In 1738 the Frenchman, La Condamine, traveled from Quito to Lima to make financial arrangements in favor of the expedition that was measuring the shape of the earth. En route he passed through Loja and made the first botanical description of the cinchona tree—a century after its discovery. He sent his observations to Linnaeus who designated the plant *cinchona officinalis.*

After Mutis's arrival to Nueva Granada in 1763, he received a sample of cinchona from the administrator of the Spanish crown's monopoly on cinchona commerce. He likewise sent these samples to Linnaeus. During the early years of the Botanical Expedition, in Mariquita, Mutis tried to establish a cinchona plantation but this was cut short by the expedition's forced return to Bogotá.

Mutis's training as a physician and a botanist made him ideally suited to decipher the mystery surrounding the use of the different species. According to one of his biographers, Mutis was the "quinologist" with the best location in the world and the most active in tests and investigations.[6] The route to discovery, however, was laden with pitfalls.

First, the harvesting and commerce of the cinchona bark were anti-technical and chaotic. The harvesters tended to be untrained laborers who often would fell trees different than the cinchona or bring back parts other than the bark. This was not well dried before packing and often different species of cinchona were mixed indiscriminately. Second, the application of the drug was haphazard. There were no systematic studies of its uses and the dosage was a matter left to each physician.

Furthermore, fortune was not in Mutis's favor. In 1772, while traveling near Bogotá, he came across a species of cinchona. Although this was the first discovery of the tree north of the equator, Mutis made no formal publication. However, a Panamean physician, Sebastian Lopez Ruiz, who had gained Mutis's confidence, claimed the discovery as his own. As a result, Lopez Ruiz traveled to Spain where he was befriended by Casimiro Ortega, director of the Jardín Botánico de Madrid (and an antagonist of Mutis). The Panamean was named to the Real Academia Médica in Madrid and given a paid position to direct that city's quinine commerce with Bogotá.

Mutis reacted in an unpriestly manner. He used his friendship with Viceroy (and Archbishop) Caballero, his patron in the establishment of the Botanical Expedition, to counterattack. Together they managed to convince the Spanish court of Mutis's priority. They pressed on until Lopez Ruiz was removed from his position, stripped of his salary, retired from the scientific societies and forced to take up residence in Peru.

Mutis eventually gained control of the cinchona commerce. He insisted on commercializing the local species (with the aid of José Ignacio Pombo in Cartagena) and began shipments in 1787. Much to his dismay Spanish physicians declared the remedy to be ineffective and by 1790 the commerce was ordered closed. This was a shocking defeat for Mutis, diminishing his reputation as a botanist. But Mutis persisted and in 1794 wrote *El Arcano de la Quina*, a treatise devoted to distinguishing the different species of cinchona and their medicinal effects.

---

6 Florentino Vezga. *La Expedición Botánica.* Carvajal and Cia. Cali. 1971, p. 44.

The controversy had become as much a matter of personalities as of science. Casimiro Ortega and his son-in-law Hipólito Ruiz (of the Peruvian Expedition) were pitted against Mutis and the members of the expedition in Nueva Granada. Thus, Mutis insisted on explaining his position to Humboldt in 1801 and the Prussian responded by supporting Mutis on the matter of his discovery of cinchona near Bogotá.

As time passed, Mutis regained lost terrain and by 1803 had sent his nephew Sinforoso to Cuba with a shipment of cinchona for sale. However, the controversy continued with a new attack by Hipólito Ruiz in 1801 and a defense issued by Mutis's former second-in-command Francisco Antonio Zea.

CALDAS TAKES PART

The advances, setbacks and intrigues associated with the cinchona problem had not made much of an impact on Caldas prior to his joining the expedition. He had been trained as a lawyer, not a physician like Mutis, and he was never to enter the clinical side of the issue. The hurried training Caldas received from Bonpland apparently did not include any special emphasis on the cinchona tree. Thus when he outlined his program of investigation to his mentor he made no mention of the cinchona issue—one of utmost importance to Mutis.

It is clear, though, that Mutis patiently and persistently impressed upon his pupil the salient points of the matter. By November 1802, five months after his formal appointment, Caldas made his first comment regarding cinchona and noted the importance of a field trip to Loja. Caldas also acknowledged Mutis's personal motives, "You tell me it is necessary to arrange a complete collection of cinchona to respond to the attacks against you by Ortega."[7]

Caldas asked for a copy of Zea's memoir and another defense written by Mutis's trusted lieutenant, Salvador Rizo. The lack of correspondence owing to Mutis's failing health and Caldas's discomforts following his trip to Malbucho delayed his turning to the cinchona problem. But, by the end of 1803 Caldas was thoroughly infused with the spirited rivalry against Ortega and the Peruvian expedition, and wrote to Mutis with that mercurial intensity that characterized him, that he wished to travel to Loja to arrive ahead of a supposed expedition from the Peruvian group, "I am so obsessed on this point that I will carry it through even if it costs me my life."[8]

Mutis was equally anxious for the outing and for some data that would be of use. Caldas, having been severely chastised for his independence, was eager to right himself with his mentor. So in January 1804 it was agreed that Caldas should travel immediately to Loja and then return

---

[7] Eduardo Posada, ed. *Cartas de Caldas.* Biblioteca de Historia Nacional. Volume 15. Imprenta Nacional. Bogotá. 1917, p. 196.
[8] Ibid., 222.

without delay with his samples to Bogotá, but that was complicated by a relapse of his illness and Mutis once again grew silent. Finally, in July 1804, Caldas, still ill, decided to leave for Loja having received only second-hand information from Mutis via Salvador Rizo and Santiago Arroyo.

After the first leg of his journey Caldas stopped in the town of Cuenca where he complained, "I arrived . . . assailed by this illness. . . . I have passed ten days amidst vomit and quinine."[9]

Caldas persisted and arrived in Loja in October 1804. He stayed in the province until the end of the year and then returned to Quito where he wrote a memoir,[10] his only publication regarding cinchona, between January and March 1805.

Along the route to Loja and in earlier field trips, Caldas had collected numerous samples of different cinchona species which can be listed as follows:

Date	Place
July 1803	Malbucho
October 1803	Intac
June 1804	Tagualo
August 1804	Alausi
September 1804	Cuenca
October/November 1804	Loja

Caldas reported enthusiastically to Mutis:

I have found and described sixteen species [Mutis recognized only four. Today there are reported to be thirty-eight[11]]. I found ten in Loja; three in Cuenca; two in Alausi; and one in Tagualo. I believe that I have exhausted the study of cinchona in this province, following your orders, and procuring that for my part may be diminished the melancholy in which you say you have fallen.[12]

Caldas stayed in the province long enough to study it well. With a population of about two thousand at the time Loja was "a group of poorly built houses, in the middle of an unequal and thin valley which extends from north to south some three or four leagues."[13]

He set about organizing plant skeletons and making drawings; speaking with the local agent for cinchona commerce; and doing what interested him most—establishing geographical limits for the different species. Indeed, Caldas drew a map generalizing his measurements. It is worth noting that he was willing to accept Hipólito Ruiz's southern limit to complement his own estimate of the northern limit. As for the alti-

---

[9] Ibid., 240.

[10] "Memoria sobre el estado de las quinas en general y en particular sobre la de Loja" in *Obras Completas de Franciso José de Caldas*. Universidad Nacional de Colombia. Imprenta Nacional. Bogotá. 1966.

[11] *Encyclopedia Britannica*. Volume 5.

[12] Eduardo Posada, ed. *Cartas de Caldas*. Biblioteca de Historia Nacional. Volume 15. Imprenta Nacional. Bogotá. 1917, p. 246.

[13] *Obras Completas de Franciso José de Caldas*. Universidad Nacional de Colombia. Imprenta Nacional. Bogotá. 1966, p. 242.

tude, Caldas took to task both Humboldt and Juan Tafalla, for he found cinchona, he said,

above the upper limit determined by Baron von Humboldt. If Tafalla with his glorious "quina" has corrected the lower limit, we alter the upper limit, and the zone of cinchona established by that traveller is of much greater extension than that published in the Geography of Plants [by Humboldt]. It is certain that Tafalla understands nothing of altitudes and if that limit is altered [the lower] it will be after we have observed it in Guayaquil.[14]

Caldas's keen interest in establishing the viability of a plant geography had a practical objective—the ability to predict where a given plant could or could not be cultivated. This seemed particularly worthwhile with regard to cinchona because as Caldas noted, "Whatever be the cause, it is certain that we do not have one cinchona tree of Loja in all the rest of the viceroyalty."[15]

In his memoir, Caldas insisted on the need to cultivate cinchona. He estimated that about ten percent of the province's supply was depleted, and criticized the destructive harvesting methods used. He suggested that plantations (some 10,000 trees) be established in other zones geographically similar to Loja (such as Popayán) since neither the residents, nor the local botanist were interested and that, technically speaking ". . . in October 1804 things are as they were at the time of its [the cinchona bark's] discovery."[16]

FURTHER DISCUSSION

Caldas held great expectations for his cinchona memoir. His patron in Quito, Baron Carondelet, commissioned a copy. Caldas complied and asked Carondelet to send a copy to Spain with a recommendation for an official position with the expedition. He also sent copies to Mutis and Pombo, expecting their approval. Pombo was critical though, noting that "his cinchona memoir is written in haste and as such has its errors."[17]

Pombo specifically criticized Caldas's geographical limits and his judgment that the Loja species was necessarily superior. There was something more to Pombo's criticisms, though—he was also at work on a memoir about the cinchona problem. (The memoir is lost.) Pombo fancied himself an expert on the matter and showed more than a little jealousy. He was probably piqued by Mutis's urgent call to Caldas to return to Bogotá, since Mutis treated Caldas as his stellar student.

In his memoir, Caldas emphasized commercial aspects and the application of his ideas on plant geography to the cinchona problem. He

---

[14] Ibid., 482.

[15] Ibid., 249.

[16] Ibid., 252.

[17] Guillermo Hernandez de Alba, ed., *Archivo Epistolar Del Sabio Naturalista Don José Celestino Mutis*. Four Volumes. Instituto Colombiano de Cultura Hispánica. Bogotá. 1983. Volume IV, p. 141.

intended to deal with cinchona in greater detail in Bogotá where he could work with his collections, and he often mentioned that he was preparing a major work on the subject. Unfortunately, here again Caldas was unable to deliver. When he arrived in the capital he was assigned to the Observatory and it was Mutis who supposedly dealt with botany. Mutis's advanced age in combination with his tendency to procrastinate did not permit any progress to be made until after the Spaniard's death in 1808.

Caldas never did publish his proposed treatise on cinchona, but he did collaborate with Sinforoso Mutis on a posthumous edition of the elder Mutis's writings. The death of Mutis, the upheaval of the revolution, the Spanish reconquest and the closure of the Botanical Expedition put the quinine commerce beyond the grasp of the Granadians, and the Dutch East Indies eventually surpassed the newly independent Latin America as the world's foremost producer of the "divine and bitter remedy."

AT HOME IN THE OBSERVATORY
1806–1810

Following three long years (1802–1805) in the mountains and jungles of Ecuador, Caldas left Quito and journeyed to Santa Fe de Bogotá. His arrival in the capital of the viceroyalty was accompanied by great expectations. Caldas's mentor, benefactor and director, Mutis, was eager to study the collections from Ecuador, especially the samples of cinchona. Mutis was also anxious for Caldas to take charge of the Astronomical Observatory which had been completed in 1803 (Fig. 9).

Caldas returned to Bogotá in conditions that he could not have imagined when he first wrote to Mutis. He directed the first astronomical observatory built in Spanish America, and it would not be much of an exaggeration to say that the Observatory had been built for Caldas. Furthermore, Mutis's reception seemed convincing proof that Caldas was already chosen to succeed his mentor as director of the botanical expedition.

Caldas established a regular program of observations in astronomy. He made meteorological measurements and encouraged others to do the same. He took on private students, made friends and expressed his opinions on the need to support the scientific community in Nueva Granada.

As Caldas's self-confidence grew, Mutis's health waned. The two men drew apart, not because of personal animosity, but owing to differences in age and expectations. While Mutis tried to put his intellectual house in order, Caldas was not allowed to advance research on his own plant specimens.

But Caldas was too energetic and ambitious to allow this vacuum to exist. He became the motive force behind the publication of a weekly periodical—El Semanario del Nuevo Reino de Granada. This was essentially a scientific journal. Under Caldas's guidance the nature and geography of the viceroyalty were amply discussed. In addition, the periodical was a platform from which he could advance his own ideas on matters of science.

In September 1808 Mutis passed away. He had determined that the botanical expedition would pass with him, by skillfully devising an intellectual testament which left Caldas as an independent director of the Observatory but did not give him the directorship of the expedition—the prize Caldas coveted most.

Although Caldas viewed Mutis's bequest as a promise broken, he eventually overcame his indignation. A triumvirate was left to carry on the expedition's work: Sinforoso Mutis, Salvador Rizo, and Caldas. They

FIGURE 9.   Drawing of the Astronomical Observatory. Reprinted from Alfredo D. Bateman. *El Observatorio Astronómico de Bogotá*. Universidad Nacional de Colombia. Bogotá. 1953.

managed to develop a working relationship as they moved forward with the study of the natural world in Nueva Granada. Caldas found a moment of tranquility and sustenance in his pursuit of science—a calm that lasted only until the revolution began.

VII. THE HEIR APPARENT

After the completion of his field trip to Loja in search of cinchona specimens, Caldas set about ordering his collections for the journey to Santa Fe de Bogotá. From late in 1803 Mutis had urged his disciple to collect cinchona specimens and return to the capital of the viceroyalty. Caldas's other patron, Pombo, began in late 1804 to press him to leave Quito, for Pombo was unable to maintain economic support for his countryman. And Caldas himself had become weary of his work in the field. Laboring in the Ecuadorean Andes virtually by himself, he had suffered the rigors of mountainous and tropical terrains, fought off illness and managed with a limited budget. He had accumulated an ample collection of specimens and maintained notebooks filled with raw data. Caldas looked forward to a period of tranquility in Bogotá in order to organize that material.

Since the journey through the mountainous "cordillera" region from Quito to Bogotá would be slow, Caldas hoped to make good use of his time. He continued to make geographical measurements and search for cinchona. He insisted that Mutis send new thermometers to continue his hypsometric observations and asked for funds to pursue investigations near his native Popayán, where he arrived on 19 May 1805. He remained in Popayán until at least September of the same year.

Pombo, though, unwilling to accept more delays, wrote to Mutis, "I told my countryman Caldas to leave aside all these projects, get on the road and go there (Bogotá), for that is what you desire and is the most convenient for many reasons."[1]

Caldas dutifully obeyed. On 10 December 1805 he arrived in Santa Fe de Bogotá with his pack animals bearing a treasure of material for the Botanical Expedition:

An herbarium of between 5,000 and 6,000 dried plant skeletons.
Two volumes of plant descriptions.
Drawings of plants by Caldas.
Seeds and bark.
Two volumes of astronomical observations.
Meteorological observations.
Geographical measurements for a map of the viceroyalty and for maps of plant geography.
Profiles of the Andes through a zone of 9° in latitude.
Specimens of animals, birds and minerals.
Two volumes of travel notes.

---

[1] Guillermo Hernandez de Alba, ed. *Archivo Epistolar Del Sabio Naturalista Don José Celestino Mutis.* Four Volumes. Instituto Colombiano de Cultura Hispánica. Bogotá. 1983. Volume IV, p. 140.

AN OBSERVATORY BUILT FOR ONE MAN

Caldas had been in Bogotá twice before. In 1788 he came to the capital as a student of law, his interest in the sciences apparently dormant. In 1796 he made the difficult journey through the "cordillera" with the specific intention of starting his work as a scientist. Yet he inexplicably missed the chance to meet with Mutis and join the only scientific organization in the viceroyalty—the Botanical Expedition.

When Caldas returned to Bogotá in late 1805, the panorama was spectacularly different. His talent as a scientist had been acknowledged by Humboldt. Mutis named him an "individual of merit" of the expedition three years earlier. Indeed, Caldas had lived up to expectations and came to the capital with a varied program of investigation and data necessary to carry it out.

There was, however, an even greater significance to Caldas's return. It resembled the return of the prodigal son. Mutis, whom Caldas did not hesitate to call "my father," had prepared an astronomical observatory for him and treated Caldas with all the attention that should be bestowed upon an heir apparent.

In his biography of Mutis,[2] Father Enrique Perez Arbalaez referred to the Astronomical Observatory of Santa Fe de Bogotá as "one tower for one man"[3]—a succinct description of the circumstances surrounding the construction of the Observatory. It is fair to say that if not for Caldas, the Observatory would not have been built.

Mutis deserves credit for having the vision to build the "first astronomical observatory on the South American continent."[4] He had dabbled in astronomy, but his work as a physician and director of the expedition left him with little time to develop a program of astronomical research. It is indicative of his conception of the expedition's mission that he tried to amplify its range of research to a field distant from his own.

Why Mutis diverted funds and effort from botanical research, while his "Flora de Bogotá" continued without signs of a definitive publication date is a significant question. Mutis was under heavy attack from the Peruvian expedition on the matter of cinchona. Furthermore, he worried that he was nearing the end of his life with his major works unfinished. Why then build an observatory?

The answer is that the observatory was built for one man. Construction began on 24 May 1802, a significant date. Early in the same year Humboldt met with Caldas and sent glowing reports to Mutis. The baron was impressed with Caldas's talent as an observer and had written that

[2] Enrique Perez Arbelaez. *José Celestino Mutis y la Real Expedición Botánica del Nuevo Reyno de Granada.* Instituto Colombiano de Cultura Hispánica. Bogotá. 1983.

[3] Ibid., 158.

[4] Mutis, Caldas and their biographers have referred to the Observatory in Bogota as the first on the South American continent. However, it was preceded by an observatory in Montevideo, Uruguay in 1789. See Carlos A. Etchecopar and Carlos Perez Montero, *El Primer Observatorio de Montevideo*, Montevideo, Instituto Histórico y Geográfico de Uruguay, 1955. (Professor Thomas Glick, private communication).

"Caldas is a prodigy in astronomy."[5] By April 1802 the possibility that Caldas might travel with Humboldt ended. For Mutis this meant that his disciple would stay in the viceroyalty. Mutis was foresighted enough to plan on making good use of Caldas and providing him with a stable position as well.

Mutis was delighted with the possibilities. In July 1802 he wrote to the new director of the Real Jardín Botánico de Madrid, Antonio Cavanilles:

Now, with anticipation, I implore your protecton and good graces for a meritorious aggregate [Caldas] to my Expedition whose destiny I must assure as a member alongside [Francisco Antonio] Zea and my nephew [Sinforoso Mutis]. . . . My old age obliges me to choose my successors and enjoy my chosen assistants in the final days of my life. This young man's vast instruction and talents will do honor to my election. For the moment I have him in Quito alongside Baron von Humboldt. . . . He has made himself a skillful astronomer and will discharge with honor the functions of the first observatory built in America.[6]

Mutis funded the construction of the Observatory with the sale of cinchona bark in Cuba where his nephew Sinforoso was at work. Final payment was made by his estate, however, after Mutis's death. Construction ended on 30 August 1803. The Observatory, situated alongside the headquarters of the Botanical Expedition, awaited its director.

There was more, though, than the honor of being named director of the Observatory; Mutis also gave his disciple the impression that the question of succession as director of the Botanical Expedition was resolved. Caldas was the heir apparent.

Soon after his arrival in Bogotá, Caldas wrote to his friend Antonio Arboleda in Popayán, "More than one envies my fortune in Santa Fe [Bogotá], more than one believes Mutis to be unjust in having preferred me instead of his nephew [Sinforoso Mutis] and all are shocked by his successor."[7]

Caldas was not showing provincial naiveté. He had good reason to believe he was Mutis's chosen successor. In an account of his introduction to Viceroy Amar y Borbon on 9 February 1806, Caldas quoted Mutis as having announced:

I [Mutis] have passed seventy-five years spent in the progress of science; my strength lessens and my work increases. To protect my sovereign, my nation and my honor I have procured a support, a cane for my old age, a man in which to deposit my discoveries and my knowledge, a man to be my confidant, my consolation and my support, and heir to my knowledge such as it is. This is don F.J. de Caldas, who is in the presence of Your Excellency and who I have the honor of presenting. For the past four years I have had him in the Province of

5 Jorge Arias de Greiff. "El Diario Inedito de Humboldt." *Revista de la Academia Colombiana de Ciencias Exactas, Fisicas y Naturales.* Volume 13. Number 51. 1969, p. 393.
6 Guillermo Hernandez de Alba, ed. *Archivo Epistolar Del Sabio Naturalista Don José Celestino Mutis.* Four Volumes. Instituto Colombiano de Cultura Hispánica. Bogotá. 1983. Volume II, p. 186.
7 Eduardo Posada, ed. *Cartas de Caldas.* Biblioteca de Historia Nacional. Volume 15. Imprenta Nacional. Bogotá. 1917, p. 297.

Quito and have now called him to my side. I implore the protection of Your Excellency to convey my wishes to the illustrious Minister of the Indies and that I may die with the consolation of having left a successor who will sustain the nation's honor and my reputation.[8]

I think that Caldas can be believed in his report of Mutis's declaration. He had nothing to gain by embellishing the truth or misleading his friend Arboleda, to whom he confided the story. In addition, I think Mutis is to be believed when he referred to Caldas as his "successor," but there is one qualifying note to Mutis's words. The "successor" had been chosen to "sustain the nation's honor and my reputation." Caldas would have done well to try to understand his mentor's intentions.

ASTRONOMY

The position of director of the Astronomical Observatory of Santa Fe de Bogotá carried no job description. Caldas was left to develop his own programs and had to work virtually without assistance. Although he had come to Bogotá to take his place in the Botanical Expedition, he encountered, instead, a certain degree of isolation:

I find myself in average health enclosed in the observatory and dedicated to the contemplation of the skies, to this dome that publishes at every moment the glory of its author. I am happy in this solitude, nothing obscures a retreat based on sublime and virtuous knowledge.[9]

The Observatory's octagonal tower was located in the garden of the Botanical Expedition. Caldas's first job was to take account of the physical plant and the instruments at his disposition. Some equipment had been supplied by the Spanish government: a quarter circle, theodolites, chronometers, thermometers and compasses; Mutis had acquired other instruments: three reflecting telescopes, octants, thermometers, barometers, compasses and a pendulum; and Caldas also contributed the quarter circle purchased from Humboldt, a theodolite, a sextant and ephemerides.

Caldas marked the north-south meridian line and began measuring the position of sun and stars to determine the Observatory's location.[10] He continued to emphasize the use of astronomical observations to obtain geographical data. In 1807 he spent several weeks reducing the data in his astronomical notebooks, principally the eclipses of the moon and the occultations of the satellites of Jupiter. This provided him with the values of longitude of the different towns in the viceroyalty he had visited. His measurement of the meridian altitude of stars, and observations of the solstices gave Caldas data with which to deduce the latitude

---

[8] Ibid., 248.

[9] Ibid., 246.

[10] Caldas's measurements of latitude (4° 36′ 6″ N) and altitude (2,686.33 meters) compare favorably with modern values—latitude = 4° 35′ 56.57″ N: altitude = 2,624.88 meters.

of these places. His goal was vast and ambitious—to map the entire vice-royalty. Caldas's geographic endeavors will be discussed further in the following chapter.

Another program to which Caldas dedicated himself was the measurement of the refraction of starlight by the atmosphere. Atmospheric refraction[11] causes a change in the observed position of a star. The effect is weaker at higher altitudes and depends on the density of the atmosphere through which starlight must pass.

This was a particularly apt problem for Caldas who was fascinated by the way changes in altitude affect different phenomena. The French Expedition had dealt with the matter. Humboldt was also interested in atmospheric refraction and certainly he and Caldas must have had occasion to discuss the subject. Caldas presented a memoir on atmospheric refraction to Viceroy Amar y Borbon in 1809. In fact, he promised the viceroy a total of three volumes describing his work. This material, unfortunately, seems to have been lost.

Caldas suggested that the location of the Observatory was ideal for developing a star catalogue of the southern hemisphere. There is little evidence to clarify how much time he dedicated to this. Caldas made constant efforts to obtain star catalogues and ephemerides. It may be that a lack of adequate references dissuaded him from embarking on this project.

Still, Caldas was an active observer. In 1807 a comet appeared in the sky. Caldas described his observations:

It is true that for more than a month this new star has occupied my time, and I believe that I shall not leave it until it has disappeared completely. There is not enough time to calculate all the elements of my observations, but they will be seen in time. Since its appearance it has constantly diminished in diameter and intensity. The tail, which was inclined to the ecliptic on the 23rd of September is now reversed and points to the North. The fan that was formed has opened more; it was seen in Virgo, passed the equator between the 28th and 29th of September . . . touched the head of the Serpent and is now (November 6, 1807) upon the back of Hercules. Who knows where it will disappear![12]

Caldas's observation of the comet was not without its difficulties, for he later wrote, "My head suffered with the comet and I am now recovering."[13]

He maintained extensive diaries of his astronomical observations. Humboldt was able to judge Caldas's aptitude for astronomy by reviewing the notes he left with his father in Popayán. When he returned to Bogotá in 1805 Caldas brought with him two volumes of data. And in his report to Viceroy Amar y Borbon in 1809, Caldas announced that he was organizing the observations which he had begun in 1797 and including

[11] See note #21, chapter 4.

[12] Eduardo Posada, ed. *Cartas de Caldas*. Biblioteca de Historia Nacional. Volume 15. Imprenta Nacional. Bogotá. 1917, p. 254.

[13] Ibid., 259.

those made in the observatory. As noted, these works are lost. Caldas never published any summary of his astronomical labors.

Despite the prestige of being director of the Observatory and the investment made in building and equipment, Caldas found it difficult to build a research program in astronomy. He worked in isolation, he had no contact with other astronomers; only sporadically could he obtain ephemerides, and he had no assistants. Caldas remarked, "I could never obtain a co-observer and I have found myself in the unfortunate situation of teaching some principles of astronomy to my servant."[14]

His astronomy was dependent upon the information available to him. For example, in his Almanac for 1812 Caldas attributed to the solar system twelve primary planets including Uranus, which Caldas referred to as "Herschel"; and four asteroides which Caldas referred to as planets named "Piazzi," "Olbers," "Hercules" and "Harding." The isolation imposed by Spain on its colonies and the upheaval caused by Napoleon's adventures in Europe denied Caldas the communication with other astronomers and observatories that would have allowed him to develop his own talents and the Observatory's potential.

Meteorology and Other Matters

The Observatory, in Caldas's conception, was not meant to deal only with astronomy. Rather, he continued to work on a variety of subjects as he had since he initiated his scientific career. The principal differences between his labors near Popayán and in Ecuador, and in his new position as the director of an institution were twofold. First, he no longer practiced itinerant science. His mission was to develop a program for the Observatory, *in* the Observatory. This suited him since he had a great amount of data and voluminous collections to organize. Caldas also felt that he had suffered considerable hardship during his field work in Ecuador. He welcomed the comfort and tranquility available in his new setting.

Second, Caldas found himself somewhat removed from the botanical activities of the expedition. He had turned his collections over to Mutis. The aging Spaniard made little effort to involve Caldas in the preparation of materials for the projected "Flora de Bogotá." Mutis apparently felt that Caldas had enough work to do with the night sky.

It was natural, then, that Caldas should develop a program of meteorological observations to complement his astronomical program. As a traveler, Caldas habitually made note of climatological conditions in each village he passed. In the Observatory he recorded measurements of barometric pressure, air temperature and humidity three times each day.

Caldas did not limit his meteorological program to a series of isolated measurements. He took the initiative of exhorting others to make their own observations. In his weekly periodical, the *Semanario*, (see Chapter

---

[14] *Obras Completas de Francisco José de Caldas.* Universidad Nacional de Colombia. Imprenta Nacional. Bogotá. 1966, p. 352.

VIII) he urged his readers to send their observations to him. As a result, by the end of 1808 Caldas could publish data collected by correspondents in Cartagena, Popayán and Cali. He was convinced of the need to generalize the accumulation of meteorological information in order to aid in the development of agriculture and commerce in the viceroyalty. Caldas clearly deserves credit for having anticipated the development of a structured network of meteorological stations in Colombia.

Even more importantly, the Observatory served as a haven from which Caldas began to deal with scientific problems on a different level. His new position gave him the confidence to speak out on the importance of supporting science in the viceroyalty. He began to conceive projects on a national scale. His initiative on meteorological data shows Caldas's development as a person and a scientist. He was capable, willing and anxious to demonstrate leadership—a positive attribute for the director of an observatory.

There are three other points which deserve mention in the present chapter. First, Caldas seems to have continued to some degree with his investigation of the hypsometric principle while in the Observatory (see Chapter II). He mentioned during 1809 that he was completing a new memoir on the subject.[15] This was never published though, so it is difficult to determine what sort of new information he had or how much time he spent on it.

Second, Caldas maintained his voracious appetite for information from Europe. In his calculation of the altitude of the Observatory he was delighted to have learned of a new method—by Laplace—for reducing readings of barometric pressure to altitude. He pestered the viceroy for a nautical almanac from Spain, commented on the caloric theory of heat and managed to obtain Humboldt's recently published articles.

Finally, Caldas built his own circle of friends, associates, students and admirers. Colombian writers have often emphasized Caldas's timid nature. This probably comes from Caldas's own account of the reasons for Humboldt's unwillingness to receive him as a traveling companion (see Chapter III), and from the curious story behind Caldas's marriage (see Chapter X). Yet when science was involved, or his position as a scientist, Caldas demonstrated quite another character. He could be aggressive, persuasive, haughty, abrasive and self-assured. This aspect of Caldas's personality became more apparent as he settled in at the Observatory.

---

[15] Ibid., 214.

VIII. THE *SEMANARIO*

As director of the Astronomical Observatory of Santa Fe de Bogotá, Caldas assumed a position of great prestige and responsibility. As an "individual of merit" of the Botanical Expedition to the Viceroyalty of Nueva Granada he was an important element of the most important scientific enterprise in his part of the world. Yet Caldas found it necessary to pay more attention to promoting his own career and protecting his own economic well-being.

Although Caldas held apparently official positions with the expedition and the Observatory, in fact he had received no official appointment from the Spanish government. In Bogotá he received a salary derived from Mutis's own discretionary funds. But Mutis was in failing health and Caldas's other patron, Pombo, could no longer offer assistance. Thus Caldas worried that following Mutis's death he might have no source of support.

On the other hand, prestigious though it might be, Caldas felt that his work in astronomy was of secondary importance. He was more interested in advancing his work in geographical and botanical matters and he hoped to join in the publication of the works of the expedition. Furthermore, he was frustrated with Mutis's appropriation of his own plant collection in order to put the final touches to those unfinished works — *Flora de Bogotá* and *Historia de las Quinas*. Instead of being an active collaborator with his mentor, Caldas felt that he had been abandoned to the solitude of the Observatory.

It is not surprising, then, that Caldas should have viewed his notebooks filled with data and his extensive plant collection as security for the future. In a letter to Santiago Arroyo, Caldas confided that, ". . . my geographical works, fruit of great efforts and expenses are my patrimony and my riches. . . ."[1] Furthermore, he was quite clear about his intentions, "My works will be published in due time and such that they assure my sustenance."[2]

That Caldas's work was highly regarded can be seen in two initiatives offered to him. In the latter part of 1806, less than a year after his arrival in Bogotá, the Consulado de Cartagena proposed that Caldas take up the project of searching for a more effective route to communicate the port city of Cartagena with the central Andean region of the viceroyalty and principally its capital, Santa Fe de Bogotá. This project was conceived by

---

[1] Eduardo Posada, ed. *Cartas de Caldas*. Biblioteca de Historia Nacional. Volume 15. Imprenta Nacional. Bogotá. 1917, p. 256.
[2] Ibid., 257.

Pombo. Apparently the consulado had funds available and hoped to convince Viceroy Amar y Borbon to support the idea. Certainly Pombo managed to gain Mutis's encouragement, and both men felt that the project would be beneficial to Caldas.

Caldas's answer to the Consulado, however, constituted for Pombo "an inopportune reply."[3] Though this reply is lost, Caldas probably requested more funds, time and logistical support than the consulado was willing or able to provide. At the same time Viceroy Amar declined to support the effort, most likely owing to budget limitations. The initiative was laid to rest.

Later, in the year 1808, Santiago Arroyo communicated to Caldas the interest of the Archbishop of Popayán in obtaining a new map of the episcopate. Although Caldas later offered his services, his initial reply (to Arroyo) was harsh but representative of his determination to defend his own interests:

If this bishop, these clergy, want a map I will make an exact one; but they will have to pay the astronomer who has sacrificed his health, who has suffered the criticisms and insults of those who now need me, who have a thousand times treated me as a fanatic and a madman because I worked not as a farmer or a merchant. To sum up, if these rich gentlemen do not give me one thousand pesos[4] for the map of the episcopate, I will not do it.[5]

EL SEMANARIO DEL NUEVO REINO DE GRANADA

Caldas took a concrete and positive step toward developing his own identity as a scientist and intellectual with the establishment of a weekly periodical known as *El Semanario del Nuevo Reino de Granada*. The periodical was initially financed by Caldas along with a group of friends and associates. It appeared for the first time on 1 January 1808 and lasted until 1811. Although the periodical was ". . . conceived and executed by many illustrious individuals of this capital [Bogotá],"[6] as time passed it became essentially a personal initiative of Caldas. It is particularly important to note that Caldas conceived of the *Semanario* as "a scientific periodical."[7] Certainly the Viceroyalty of Nueva Granada was not a likely place to be able to support such a weekly. Its population was dispersed and could count only the Botanical Expedition as a scientific institution. That Caldas attempted to breathe life into this enterprise might be attrib-

---

3 Guillermo Hernandez de Alba, ed. *Archivo Epistolar Del Sabio Naturalista Don José Celestino Mutis*. Four Volumes. Instituto Colombiano de Cultura Hispánica. Bogotá. 1983. Volume IV, p. 167.

4 Caldas at this point received four hundred pesos ($400) a year as Director of the Observatory.

5 Eduardo Posada, ed. *Cartas de Caldas*. Biblioteca de Historia Nacional. Volume 15. Imprenta Nacional. Bogotá. 1917, p. 259.

6 *Obras Completas de Francisco José de Caldas*. Universidad Nacional de Colombia. Imprenta Nacional. Bogotá. 1966, p. 411, footnote.

7 Ibid., 361.

uted to naiveté. I believe, however, that such an attitude would amount to selling Caldas short. He understood that communication between scientists is essential; that a nascent community in Nueva Granada needed contact with the established community in Europe; that science needs financial and moral support from the general public for its advancement; and that the public which is expected to support the scientific enterprise must be convinced of its utility.

Caldas hoped that his periodical would enlighten and inform. He believed that it was necessary to educate the public about science, and that this educated public would, in turn, support the cause of science. He was interested in emphasizing the practical, and wrote, ". . . the *Semanario* [is] dedicated principally to the utility of the Viceroyalty and to manifest the state of our territory. . . ."[8] He also wished to maintain certain standards, "The *Semanario* is a serious paper, dedicated to solid memoirs regarding the points of major interest."[9]

The "points of major interest" were those of utility to the viceroyalty. The *Semanario* was dedicated in great measure to the study of Nueva Granada. Appropriately, Caldas announced that "*El Semanario del Nuevo Reino de Granada* will begin with the state of its geography."[10]

In the first seven issues of the *Semanario*, Caldas published an article of his own "The Present State of the Geography of the Viceroyalty of Santa Fe de Bogotá with Relation to its Economy and Commerce." This constituted Caldas's geographical manifesto, wherein he showed a vast first-hand knowledge of his native land. Caldas was explicit in his conception of geography:

Geography is the fundamental basis of all political speculation; it gives the extent of the country with which one wishes to deal; teaches the relationships with the rest of the world's nations; the kindness of its coasts, its navigable rivers, the mountains which cross it, the valleys they form; the distances between towns, the established roads, those that can be opened; the climate, the temperature, the elevation of all points above sea level; the art and customs of its inhabitants; spontaneous productions and those that can be domesticated by craft.[11]

Caldas must have enjoyed immensely writing this article for it showed a mastery of the subject and radiated excitement about the prospects for the future. He dealt with a wide range of items: the borders of Nueva Granada; a clear and beautiful description of the cordillera region of the Andes from Loja to Bogotá[12]; the stone statues left by Indian artists in San Agustín; and volcanos. In this article Caldas discussed the privileged position of Nueva Granada in having both Caribbean and Pacific

---

8 Ibid., 411.
9 Ibid., 413.
10 Ibid., 183.
11 Ibid., 183.
12 For example, with regard to his home town Caldas wrote of ". . . the spacious and unequal valley of Popayán at an altitude of 900 toises and a temperature between 10° C and 18° C that seems to have been invented by poets." Ibid., 186.

coasts. He noted, "Because of its geographical position Nueva Granada appears destined for universal commerce."[13]

Indeed, he dealt with the problem of finding a connecting route between the two oceans. Along with other writers, such as Humboldt and Pombo, Caldas added to the call for action which led a century later to the construction of the Panama Canal. He exhorted the Spanish government to take positive action on the matter, "But, what have we done with these flattering expectations? We have not taken a single step on this matter; one capable of changing America's ideas of commerce."[14]

Caldas noted that some progress had been made on the study of geography in Nueva Granada, and paid special tribute to the members of the French Expedition to the Equator; to Humboldt; and to Joaquin Francisco Fidalgo, captain and chief of the expedition to study the coastal areas in the Caribbean.

Yet Caldas considered the study of geography to be just beginning in the viceroyalty and urged that all students be able to ". . . measure terrain, draw a plan, determine latitude, use a compass. . . ."[15] He projected a grandiose plan for constructing a complete and exact map of the viceroyalty. This would have been a national effort to support a geographical expedition composed of an astronomer, a botanist, a mineralogist, a zoologist, an economist and a support staff. This project never materialized, but Caldas insisted on improving the state of geographical knowledge. He asked his readers to contribute articles on the subject and warned them of ". . . miserable maps, maps without detail, contradictory maps . . ."[16] that were available.

This call was heeded by José Manuel Restrepo, a disciple of Caldas, who contributed an article on the Antioquia region; by José Joaquin Camacho, future collaborator with Caldas in the *Diario Político* (see Chapter X), who wrote on the Pamplona region; by Jorge Tadeo Lozano, member of the Botanical Expedition, who presented his work on the fauna of Cundinamarca; and others.

The *Semanario* also contributed to a general awareness of the importance of geography by publishing three articles written by Baron Alexander von Humboldt. The first of these was Humboldt's study on plant geography that the baron had sent to Mutis prior to embarking for Mexico (see Chapter V). It was published in April 1809, several months following Mutis's death. Although Caldas had made his own copy in 1803 he apparently felt that he should defer to Mutis who, Caldas noted, "maintained the original unpublished until his death. . . ."[17]

The versions published in the *Semanario* were a translation from the French original made by Caldas's colleague, Jorge Tadeo Lozano. Caldas

---

[13] Ibid., 188.
[14] Ibid., 190.
[15] Ibid., 210.
[16] Ibid., 190.
[17] Ibid., 384.

complemented the article with a commentary in which he defended Mutis, attacked the Peruvian expedition and noted his own measurements of altitude. Caldas conceded Humboldt's priority on the subject of plant geography by asserting that he carried Humboldt's article during his travels in Ecuador. However, Caldas was determined to carry out his own program on plant geography and announced that, "since several years ago we have gathered materials and observations for a work titled *Phytogeography near the Equator* basing our work on a vaster plan, perhaps more useful for commerce, agriculture and medicinal plants."[18]

Two more articles written by Humboldt were published in 1810, regarding his observations in Nueva Granada and Mexico.[19] By this point the *Semanario* was no longer a weekly publication, but appeared in the form of complete memoirs. Caldas probably received these articles, published in London, from Carlos Montufar who had traveled with Humboldt and Bonpland to Europe (see Chapter III) and returned to Nueva Granada as the political movement of 1810 advanced. In 1802 Caldas felt that Montufar had occupied a place that rightly belonged to him, but it would seem that time had indeed healed that wound.

The publication of these articles by the Prussian naturalist gave the *Semanario* a mark of quality. Caldas used the opportunity not only to comment on the contents of the works but also to urge his readers to take up meteorological observations, geographical measurements and the recording of vital statistics. Caldas was highly respectful of Humboldt's work and was always careful to give the baron proper credit.

Yet he also felt free to correct or criticize Humboldt when he thought it necessary. He regarded Humboldt's efforts as a guide to his own work, but, in no way did Caldas give the impression that European necessarily meant superior. He felt that there was much to be done in Nueva Granada and that good science could be done by the Granadians themselves. From the pages of the *Semanario* Caldas urged his contemporaries to take up the study of their own portion of America.

The Writer's Pen

There were many contributors to the *Semanario*. Caldas tried to incorporate friends, students and colleagues in his effort to establish a forum for science in the viceroyalty. The *Semanario* provided the members of the Botanical Expedition, Caldas, Jorge Tadeo Lozano, Sinforoso Mutis and former member Eloy Valenzuela, with an opportunity to publish the results of their investigations. It opened its pages to correspondents who lived outside the capital. Caldas succeeded in promoting the participation of his readers. Notes were sent regarding new plants, statistics on births and deaths in several towns were sent by local clergy. The *Semanario*

---

[18] Ibid., 385.
[19] "Estadística de Mejico." Ibid., 179 and "Cuadro físico de las regiones ecuatoriales." Ibid., 37.

published meteorological observations obtained in different parts of the colony. An account was given of the number of persons who received smallpox vaccinations. And although there were some works of literature, poetry and social notes, the *Semanario* maintained an essentially scientific orientation.

Caldas was anxious for the *Semanario* to be open to the nascent scientific community of Nueva Granada. Nevertheless, it was inevitable that the periodical should also serve as a stage for the presentation of Caldas's own work. As director of the *Semanario*, Caldas was constantly present as a writer, commentator or through notes to his readers. In the process of putting his thoughts on paper, Caldas took on a new position within the Granadian intellectual community. Having arrived an accomplished scientist in 1805, acknowledged for his talents as an astronomer, geographer and botanist, Caldas in the *Semanario* developed into a scientific generalist, respected for his opinions on matters of wide-ranging interest.

In the pages of the *Semanario*, Caldas discussed the possibility of adapting different plants and animals in the viceroyalty as a stimulus to its economy—a conception of the periodical as a forum for utilitarian science. In 1810 Caldas published two memoirs on the subject. In the first he suggested bringing from Mexico the cochineal, an insect grown on cacti and crushed when mature to produce a dye for cloth. He discussed the project from the geographical point of view, noting the altitude limits and climatic conditions that would favor cultivation of the cochineal. The promotion of this product had been dealt with thirty years earlier and Caldas obtained the technical reports commissioned by Viceroy Antonio Florez in 1776. Caldas presented a revised version of these instructions, including discussions of cacti cultivation, cochineal growth, selection, pests and harvesting, as well as processing, packing and transport.

In a similar memoir, also published in 1810, Caldas suggested the transport of thousands of vicuña, a ruminant, from Peru to establish herds in Nueva Granada. He noted that, "the vicuña is the most important product, the most useful animal, the most beneficial that man has found in the immense extension of the New Continent."[20]

Here Caldas returned to his ideas on the geographical distribution of plants, animals, and even insects. He was convinced that an aggressive plan to bring to Nueva Granada those species that were uniquely suited to its geographical situation could bring the colony economic and commercial benefits.

This fascination with the way plant and animal species were distributed throughout the world led Caldas to write that human actions were influenced by the climate or environment they inhabit. Caldas was challenged by one of his associates who read this to mean that environment determined behavior. As a result, Caldas defended, clarified and amplified his ideas in an article published in the *Semanario* in mid-1808.

---

[20] Ibid., 324.

This article, "The Influence of the Climate on Organized Beings,"[21] occupied nine issues of the *Semanario*. It was an extensive presentation that tended more toward generalization and depended less on numerical observation than any other of Caldas's writings. Yet this is the article that has captured the attention of most Colombian writers. It has even been claimed that Caldas anticipated the development of Darwinism in this publication.[22]

Initially, Caldas tried to calm his critics by accepting that there are innate and educational factors for human behavior. He was careful not to exaggerate the influence of the physical environment. He wrote, "It is true that the physical environment is influential; but only in that it increases or decreases the stimuli for the [human] machine, always leaving our will free to embrace good or evil."[23]

He included in the physical environment several factors—temperature, atmospheric pressure, atmospheric electricity, mountains, wind, rivers, jungles, rain and food. He justified his own authority on the matter by noting that:

I have observed the Andes in the neighborhood of the equator, from their base to the mansion of eternal ice; I have visited plants bathed by ocean waves, and climbed with the same objective, and always with a barometer in my hand, to the peaks of Pichincha, Corazón, Imbabura, Cotacache, Azuay, Coconuco and Guanacas; I have traveled 9° in latitude and 5° 30′ in longitude, always climbing and descending in all directions this immense and striking cordillera.[24]

Based on his experience Caldas concluded that "nature has made the physical environment for the species, and the species for the physical environment."[25] Humans, Caldas claimed, had different racial features in differences in the physical environment. He wrote, "These enormous differences, these distinctive characteristics of the people who live in the extremities of the world are nothing other than the products of heat and cold. . . ."[26]

According to Caldas, temperature extremes affected man's behavior negatively. He regarded European society—in the temperate zone—as superior to both African (hot) and Eskimo (cold) civilizations. He discussed the distribution of African and Indian descendants along the Andes and was convinced that, as plant species preferred special habitats so, too, were the different human races products of their points of origin.

Caldas, of course, never traveled to Africa or the North Pole. Nor did

---

[21] Although Caldas used the word "clima" which means "climate" and not "ambiente" which means "environment," I think that "physical environment" is, in fact, closer to his meaning and will use it in the present discussion.

[22] Alvaro Fernandez. "Del Influjo del Clima sobre los Seres Organizados." in *Estado Actual de la Investigación sobre Caldas*. Universidad del Cauca. Popayán. 1986.

[23] *Obras Completas de Francisco José de Caldas*. Universidad Nacional de Colombia. Imprenta Nacional. Bogotá. 1966, p. 82.

[24] Ibid., 103.

[25] Ibid., 89.

[26] Ibid., 86.

he observe flora and fauna other than that of Nueva Granada. He was, however, an avid reader of travel diaries and books on natural history. In the *Semanario* he felt confident enough to part from the details of barometric and astronomical measurements and take on the problem of why life was distributed as it was on the face of the Earth.

THE PRACTICAL SIDE OF THINGS

The *Semanario* was not the first periodical published in the Viceroyalty of Nueva Granada. Earlier offerings included *Papel Periodico Ilustrado* and *Correo Curioso*. In the latter Caldas made his debut in 1801 with his article on the height of the Guadalupe and Monserrate peaks (see Chapter I). *Correo Curioso* had been organized by Jorge Tadeo Lozano, a well-to-do member of the Botanical Expedition. By the time Caldas arrived in Bogotá to assume his duties in the Observatory, this periodical had stopped publishing.

Certainly Caldas must have been aware of the difficulties he would encounter in trying to establish a scientific periodical. It is a credit to his tenacity that he managed to keep it alive as long as he did. Although there is little material available on the day-to-day operation of the *Semanario*, Caldas's letters indicate that problems appeared early on. The *Semanario* began publication in January 1808, but by July of the same year Caldas wrote to his friend Arroyo to complain, "If I were not in charge I believe that this beautiful establishment now would have come undone."[27]

Caldas evidently felt that much of what was published was not particularly substantive. He was hopeful that "perhaps the Semanario will fall in my hands next year. . . ."[28]

The shake-out occurred quickly, and, in August 1808, a separata was published in which it was announced that the periodical would become essentially a two-man operation—Caldas and the printer. As publishing operations were simplified, science was intensified. Caldas called on his readers for articles regarding geography, meteorology, agriculture, botany and commerce. The initial enthusiasm was on the wane. Caldas wrote to Arroyo in January 1809, "I fear that the *Semanario* will close for lack of subscriptions, as they do not yet reach fifty. If they do not increase within a month this will end as all things do in Santa Fe [Bogotá]."[29]

He persevered, however, and published throughout 1809. At the year's end the *Semanario* could report earnings of $1,034 pesos and expenses of $1,000 pesos. The surplus of 34 pesos was to be divided between Caldas and the printer, but Caldas ceded his part. He summed up in 1809, saying,

[27] Eduardo Posada, ed. *Cartas de Caldas*. Biblioteca de Historia Nacional. Volume 15. Imprenta Nacional. Bogotá. 1917, p. 263.
[28] Ibid., 264.
[29] Ibid., 265.

"I have passed an entire year, spending my time, my paper and my health for the public."[30]

Following two years of weekly publication, Caldas decided on drastic reforms. The periodical would no longer publish weekly, but approximately monthly. It would publish complete articles and not fragments. And Caldas made it clear that he intended to maintain a high level of scholarship, even if that meant losing subscribers:

To avoid these inconveniences and so that none may claim to have been fooled we declare that the *Semanario* will contain works on economy, agriculture, science and literature. He who is not sufficiently enlightened to understand these subjects should not subscribe and favor us by avoiding the unpleasantness of the criticisms and defamations which have so plagued us in the past year.[31]

In this format publication continued into 1811. In the end, the *Semanario* was a casualty of the revolution of 1810, for the newly independent nation had little time or money to sustain a scientific periodical.

During its existence the *Semanario* contributed not only to the cultural milieu of Nueva Granada but to Caldas's personal growth as well. He had taken on the identity of an intellectual, a leader of the scientific enterprise. He enjoyed a stable and visible position in the community. And, in addition, Caldas came to regard the work of a writer/editor/publisher as a possible source of support for an uncertain future.

30 Ibid., 368.
31 *Obras Completas de Francisco José de Caldas.* Universidad Nacional de Colombia. Imprenta Nacional. Bogotá. 1966, p. 361.

IX. THE EXPEDITION TRANSFORMED

The establishment of the Botanical Expedition was part of the coming of the Enlightenment to the Spanish Empire. And José Celestino Mutis had a broad conception of what the expedition should do. He was not only interested in cataloging new plants, he tried to build an institution which extended itself into many areas. Mutis took an interest in education in the viceroyalty; built the Astronomical Observatory; maintained correspondence with persons throughout the colony; trained painters; educated young scientists; and supported the colonists' interest in developing their agriculture, commerce and culture. Because he had spent twenty years seeking support from the Spanish government for the expedition, and because he spent more than twenty years making it a reality, Mutis maintained a highly personalized vision of *his* expedition.

Caldas worked almost independently as director of the Observatory. Furthermore, the *Semanario* was an equally independent initiative. Yet, Caldas was undoubtedly part of the extended, though somewhat diffuse, zone of influence of the expedition. And although he may have been the most brilliant of Mutis's disciples, he was by no means the only star in his mentor's constellation.

Among the many members, ex-members, honorary members, correspondents, students and friends of the Botanical Expedition it is worthwhile to present here the background of those who were most important to Caldas in one way or another.

From the beginning of the expedition, Mutis maintained at his side a second-in-command. The first of these was Eloy Valenzuela who, like Mutis, was a priest and a botanist. Valenzuela worked with the newly formed expedition in 1783 and 1784. He then took charge of the Archdiocese of Bucaramanga but continued to study plant life. Valenzuela maintained correspondence with Mutis and served as tutor to his nephew, Sinforoso. Valenzuela took Caldas to task with regard to the *Semanario* as we shall see later on.

When the expedition left Mariquita and set up shop in Bogotá in 1791, Francisco Antonio Zea joined as scientific associate. Zea worked on botanical matters under Mutis's direction until 1795 when he was implicated in the scandal caused by the publication of the *Rights of Man* (see Chapter X). He was sent to Spain for imprisonment but in 1799 was declared innocent. Zea's expatriation turned out to be a stroke of luck as he was later able to study chemistry in Paris and join the Jardín Botánico de Madrid as assistant to the director, Antonio Cavanilles. Zea sided with Mutis in the cinchona dispute (see Chapter VI). Upon Cavanilles's death in 1804, Zea assumed the position of director of the Jardín Botánico.

Caldas was hopeful of obtaining an appointment to the position vacated by Zea.

Salvador Rizo joined the expedition as a painter but rose quickly to become director of all painters, treasurer of the expedition and Mutis's right hand man. From Caldas's letters we know that he corresponded often with Rizo, especially during Mutis's periods of illness. Evidently Mutis trusted Rizo and depended upon him for the day-to-day operation of the expedition.

Sinforoso Mutis y Consuegra was a nephew to José Celestino Mutis. When Sinforoso's father passed away, his uncle took it upon himself to be his nephew's protector. Sinforoso studied with Valenzuela and joined the expedition in Bogotá. Like Zea, he was implicated in the *Rights of Man* scandal. And like Zea, he made use of his expatriation to Spain to further his studies. Sinforoso returned to Nueva Granada in 1802. His uncle then sent him to Cuba where Sinforoso studied flora and sold cinchona. Caldas maintained cordial relations with Sinforoso Mutis despite the fact that both were considered possible successors to the elder Mutis.

Jorge Tadeo Lozano was a member of the Spanish nobility who moved to America. Having studied chemistry, mineralogy and botany in Spain, he was officially appointed to the expedition as zoologist in 1803 but worked ad honorem. His main interest was the Fauna of Cundinamarca and published on the subject in the *Semanario*. Caldas often referred in his letters to the presence of Lozano in the Observatory, which seems to indicate that they were friends as well as collaborators.

The efforts of the expedition were focused on finishing Mutis's works— *Flora de Bogotá* and *Historia de la Quina*. The painters, under Rizo's direction, were dedicated to completing the drawings for these projects. In Spain there was, at least, the moral support of Zea. The Botanical Expedition that Caldas encountered when he took charge of the Observatory was certainly an institution full of vitality. The citizens of Nueva Granada were anxious to see science develop along with their colony. Indeed, with the careful approval of Mutis, the members of the expedition were in the forefront of the awakening of Granadian national fervor.

A Scientific Testament

José Celestino Mutis died on 11 September 1808. His passing was not unexpected as he had been in failing health for a number of years. At the time of his death Mutis was attended by his disciples—Salvador Rizo, Sinforoso Mutis, Jorge Tadeo Lozano and Caldas who published an eloquent obituary in the *Semanario*.

The problem of how the expedition would continue after his death had preoccupied Mutis. He worked out an exact plan and communicated this from his deathbed to Viceroy Amar y Borbon, via Salvador Rizo, whom Mutis had named executor. In this "scientific testament" Mutis found an elegant solution, from his viewpoint, to the problem. In simplest terms, Mutis's bequest stipulated that 1) the position of director of the Botanical Expedition be abolished; and 2) that the expedition be divided in three sections, each with an independent director, those being Caldas, Sinforoso Mutis and Salvador Rizo.

Caldas was dumbfounded, deceived and dismayed. As when Baron von Humboldt refused his company in Quito, Caldas's mercurial temperament shot out of control.

Ever since his arrival in Bogotá, Caldas maintained the conviction that Mutis had signaled him out as the chosen successor. The position of director of the expedition was terribly important for Caldas because of the prestige, economic security and scientific independence that it seemed to offer. Mutis's triumvirate solution, then, was a direct blow to Caldas's aspirations.

Mutis's bequest was not the final word, though. The expedition was a creation of the Spanish government and, as such, was subject to the authority of the viceroy. Cautious and somewhat plodding, Viceroy Amar set about the task of reorganization. He tended to accept Mutis's testament but appointed his secretary to prepare a report on the state of things. Thus while Caldas in mid-September 1808 praised Mutis in the *Semanario*, at the end of the month he complained to the Viceroy's secretary that "this sage [Mutis] continually nurtured me with expectations and offers that he knew not how to fulfill while he lived."[1]

The triumvirate created by Mutis gave each man well-defined responsibilities and limitations. Sinforoso Mutis was given control over botanical matters, including the plant collections and paintings already completed. As a practical matter he was to complete his uncle's unfinished works. By being named director of the botanical section, however, young Mutis was considered José Celestino Mutis's successor. Salvador Rizo was to continue his work as usual—director of painters and the expedition's bookkeeper. But, he was independent of the other two directors, thus giving him equal stature. For Caldas it was also business as usual except that he likewise became autonomous in his position as director of the Observatory.

In his letter to the viceroy's secretary, Caldas noted that he had been admitted to the expedition as an "individual of merit" ('individuo meritorio') and not as an astronomer. Caldas argued that Mutis had assigned him primarily to work as a botanist. He claimed that his cinchona collection had "extended Mutis's knowledge"[2] of the tree. Indeed, Caldas asserted that

I have seen all the species of cinchona present in the viceroyalty alive and in their natural habitat, that I have studied them all carefully and that on this point I am at an advantage with respect to Mutis . . . without my work the "Quinologia" [*Historia de la Quina*] of Mutis would contain a thousand doubts and would have been reduced to half.[3]

---

[1] *Obras Completas de Francisco José de Caldas*. Universidad Nacional de Colombia. Imprenta Nacional. Bogotá. 1966, p. 352.
[2] Ibid., 350.
[3] Ibid., 350.

On the matter of plant geography Caldas was quick to note that he did not owe the idea to Mutis. With respect to the Observatory he derided Mutis for not even having unpacked the instruments. In fact, Caldas suggested that he at last had come to know the real Mutis, "But his [Mutis's] mysterious and mistrustful character, of which he could not prescind, kept him ever in silence and retreat. . . . He always kept me in ignorance of the state of things, and I have come to know them superficially after his death."[4]

Among the accusations that Caldas made of the man he once referred to as "my father" were: the plant drawings were unnumbered, the manuscripts confused, the *Flora de Bogotá* incomplete, the cinchona memoir dealt only with medicinal aspects, Mutis's works were "mere jottings,"[5] and, as if the preceding were not enough, Mutis had made barometric measurements with defective instruments. Caldas wrote, "Mutis, this man so justly praised in Europe, has not possessed a perfect barometer until I arrived."[6]

Caldas also charged that Mutis was at fault for not having secured an official position for him despite having often called Caldas, "fortunate Caldas" and "my worthy successor." Indeed, Caldas gave most credit for supporting his expedition in Ecuador to José Ignacio de Pombo. Finally, he accused Mutis of having ". . . removed me with the maximum ingratitude and injustice from the botanical section. . . ."[7]

This distasteful and excessive tirade by Caldas against his mentor contained elements of truth as well as unwarranted distortions. Caldas was correct to insist on the originality of his own work on plant geography, the value of his cinchona collections and his mastery of barometric and astronomical measurements. Furthermore, it seems that Mutis's inability to publish his findings during twenty-five years as director of the expedition would confirm Caldas's assertions of isolation and disorder.

Caldas was showing his own ingratitude by denying that it was Mutis who supported him in Ecuador. Not only did Mutis spend his own money on Caldas, he also enlisted the aid of Pombo. With regard to an official appointment for Caldas, Mutis had taken up the matter as early as 1803 with the director of the Jardín Botánico de Madrid, Antonio Cavanilles. It was Spain's difficult political situation, more than any failure on Mutis's part that had kept Caldas from obtaining official recognition.

His caustic remarks notwithstanding, Caldas was resigned to having lost the director's chair. He asked to be retained as head of the Observatory "with a moderate salary for my subsistence."[8] The only change he asked of Mutis's testament was that the plants he collected in Ecuador be returned to him so that he might organize their presentation. At least,

---

[4] Ibid., 352.
[5] Ibid., 353.
[6] Ibid., 352.
[7] Ibid., 352.
[8] Ibid., 354.

Caldas maintained enough control to vent his wrath only against the elder Mutis, and not against his nephew, saying, "I ask nothing against Sinforoso Mutis. I do not wish to raise my fortune on another man's ruin."[9]

The process of reorganizing the expedition was long and drawn out. The uncertainty weighed heavily on Caldas. In January 1809 he wrote to his friend Arroyo that no decision had yet been taken by the viceroy and complained, "My health is not the best; a thousand problems have undermined my heart and struck at my soul. You must be happy not to depend on anyone, nor expect your bread from the Viceroy's decrees."[10] Perhaps Caldas would not have been so afflicted by the process following Mutis's death if he had tried to understand his mentor's point of view. For Mutis had deftly resolved a number of difficulties by arriving at his "triumvirate solution." First, he had assured that the Botanical Expedition would be associated only with his own name by having eliminated the position of director. Second, he entrusted his unfinished works to his nephew, the person most likely to see them to completion and respect Mutis's authorship.

Mutis next gave permanent positions to three individuals for whom he felt responsible. The elder Mutis had tried to guide his nephew since the death of Sinforoso's father. When Sinforoso was taken prisoner and sent to Spain, his uncle was shocked and took an even greater interest in providing a productive, stable future. Salvador Rizo had been a loyal assistant for many years. Undoubtedly Mutis hoped that by making Rizo's position independent of the other two "heirs" possible conflict would be avoided. And although Caldas did not admit it, Mutis had made a great effort to provide him with the professional and financial stability that he needed.

Finally, Mutis managed to divide his own salary so that Sinforoso, Rizo and Caldas would all enjoy income in the new expedition of $1000 pesos per annum. The "triumvirate solution," then, gave each man equal importance, independence and salary.

The viceroy delayed for five months in making his decision. Caldas suffered in the meantime, "My state is to be lamented, my benefits—room, board, servants, candles and laundry—were withdrawn and my salary of four hundred pesos was questioned, making necessary the verdict of a judge. Without the aid of my friends I could not have survived."[11]

In the end though, Caldas was well treated. He received control of his Ecuadorean collections as he had wished. Evidently Sinforoso Mutis made no claim against him. Young Mutis was interested in finishing his uncle's work, not in imposing himself on his friend and colleague. Indeed, Caldas himself recognized that he was favored by being free to

[9] Ibid., 352.
[10] Eduardo Posada, ed. Cartas de Caldas. Biblioteca de Historia Nacional. Volume 15. Imprenta Nacional. Bogotá. 1917, p. 266.
[11] Ibid., 266.

do his own work, instead of having to decipher Mutis's manuscripts. As a further prize, Caldas assumed the professorship vacated by his mentor. In a positive tone Caldas wrote to Arroyo in March 1809: "I have been left as an independent Director of the Observatory and associated with the continuation of the *Flora de Bogotá* with one thousand pesos. I was also given, with praise, the chair of mathematics which today earns two hundred pesos. Thus, my Santiago, I have assured my bread at the age of thirty-nine, laborious years."[12]

CARRYING ON

In the months that followed, the expedition maintained its integrity as an institution. The three independent directors tried to advance their programs under the auspices of Viceroy Amar. Difficulties in Spain made new initiatives impossible. The viceroy, however, deserves credit for supporting the work of the expedition. Progress was to be found in some quarters, divisiveness in others.

Salvador Rizo resigned from the expedition in 1811 owing to a legal battle with Sinforoso Mutis over the inheritance of the profits of the elder Mutis's sale of cinchona bark in Cuba. Caldas also came under attack — from Mutis's first assistant, Father Eloy Valenzuela.

Valenzuela was angered that his works had not been published in the *Semanario* and that Caldas had not answered his letters. To present his case, Valenzuela published a pamphlet in which he derided "presumptuous graduates who sell themselves as sages."[13] Furthermore, he claimed that Caldas had misused the subscription fee that Valenzuela had sent in support of the *Semanario* and that Caldas had never sent him copies of the periodical. Valenzuela's pamphlet included a harsh judgment of the *Semanario* and its director:

Thus is Caldas; thus the *Semanario* of Santa Fe [Bogotá], and one should not be surprised that its decadence and its proximity to ruin could have been expected, or could be avoided with less partiality and more efficiency and courtesy. Humboldt's ephemeral and provisional aggregate judges himself to be above the laws of attention and correspondence, as if to be a great man consisted in being mute, not responding, in lacking urbanity and gratitude.[14]

In the face of Valenzuela's criticism Caldas kept his temper under control and tried to stay above the fray. He politely noted that he had asked Valenzuela for articles for publication and had returned the subscription fee to Valenzuela's representative. Caldas tried to put the best possible face on the matter and wrote, ". . . despite his [Valenzuela's] insults, I love him, respect him and will serve him as he wishes."[15]

Just as there was evidence of dissension in the ranks, so too was there

---

12 Ibid., 267.
13 Ibid., 364.
14 Ibid., 365.
15 Ibid., 371.

a notable vitality in the efforts to keep the expedition alive. In the year following the elder Mutis's death, Sinforoso Mutis completed the work on the cinchona tree, *Historia de los Arboles de Quina*. Caldas collaborated with the specimens and data he had collected in Ecuador. Jorge Tadeo Lozano continued work on the *Fauna de Cundinamarca* and young Mutis turned his attention to the *Flora de Bogotá*.

Caldas's program of research continued much as before. He continued to make meteorological observations, and promised a revised hypsometry memoir. In a report to Viceroy Amar y Borbon, Caldas focused on three projects:

1. A collection of astronomical observations—this was discussed in Chapter VII.
2. A memoir discussing the geographical distribution of the cinchona tree.
3. A general study of plant geography.

In the application of his concept of plant geography to the cinchona tree Caldas specified his objectives:

   i) Given a location in the equatorial Andes, determine the species of cinchona that are produced.
   ii) Given a location in the Andes, determine if there are cinchona trees in the forest or not.
   iii) Given a location in the Andes, determine which species of cinchona tree is most appropriate for cultivation.
   iv) Given the latitude of a place, determine if the cinchona tree can live there.
   v) Given the species of tree, determine in which place it will prosper most.
   vi) Calculate the area occupied by each species.
   vii) Determine the places in the viceroyalty most appropriate for the cultivation of each species.[16]

Caldas claimed to have gained support for the project from Mutis. All that was needed to begin drawing the profiles of cinchona tree distribution was one final field trip which had also been approved by Mutis.

As a third project Caldas planned a more general work "A Geography of the Plants near the Equator," in which he planned to treat a) medicinal plants; b) useful plants; and c) plants in general. To this end he had designed eighteen drawings of plant distributions against altitude profiles of the Andes. Ten of these drawings had been completed at the time of Mutis's death. The proposed field trip to the nearby Andes was also intended to complete the data needed for the profiles.

The Viceroy was supportive of Caldas but made it clear that the "calamity" of the French invasion of Spain made new expenses impos-

---

[16] *Obras Completas de Francisco José de Caldas.* Universidad Nacional de Colombia. Imprenta Nacional. Bogotá. 1966, p. 218.

sible. The field trip would have to wait, as would Caldas's request for an assistant. The Viceroy did, however, provide Caldas with a nautical almanac and some basic materials.

Caldas acceded to delay his work and noted that, "I am well aware of the urgencies and afflictions of the State in this unfortunate epoch, and I hope that once the tempest excited by the tyranny of Napoleon has calmed, our illustrious government will be able to protect useful knowledge, as it always has."[17]

He maintained his hopes of receiving an official appointment from Madrid. In June 1809 Caldas tried to enlist the support of his friends, Santiago Arroyo and Antonio Arboleda on the matter. And in March 1810 he tried to convince Antonio de Narvaez, the Viceroy's representative to Spain, to aid him in gaining recognition of his position from the Spanish government. These efforts brought no results.

Caldas and the other members of the expedition enjoyed a certain tranquility during 1809 and the first half of 1810. There was no great progress, but there was some. There were disputes, but these were not great. They even enjoyed the pleasures of mutual adulation. In the pages of the *Semanario* Sinforoso Mutis dedicated new plant species to Jorge Tadeo Lozano and Eloy Valenzuela. Caldas made his own dedications to José Ignacio de Pombo, Sinforoso Mutis and, aptly enough, to Viceroy Amar y Borbon. Although the most ambitious projects laid dormant, Caldas found enough serenity to declare, "Here [in the Observatory] I pass my days in peace, dedicated to the contemplation of great objects, so useful to society and so innocent."[18]

Unfortunately for Caldas, the days of peace and innocence were soon to come to an end.

---

[17] Ibid., 227.
[18] Ibid., 220.

LOST IN THE REVOLUTIONARY MAELSTROM
1810–1816

In the year 1810 the forces of history caught up with Caldas. As the decadent Spanish monarchy fell into Napoleon's grasp in Europe and the spirit of the age of revolution filtered through to the inhabitants of Spanish America, the call for independence from Spain became inevitable. Caldas, however, was a moderate who felt that the failures of Spanish colonialism and the just aspirations of the Spanish-Americans, or Creoles, could be reconciled without the need for armed revolution.

When in July 1810 the Creoles overthrew the colonial government in Nueva Granada, the leaders of the revolt were Caldas's friends, relatives and colleagues. Nevertheless, Caldas himself was taken by surprise. The revolution threatened the stability of his position in the Observatory and the tranquility of his recent marriage. Only after the settling of the dust did Caldas join in the revolutionary fervor, contributing with his talents as a writer and editor.

Although most of the provinces which had formed the viceroyalty of Nueva Granada were united in their desire for independence from Spain, they were unable to agree on what type of government best suited their interests. Opinion was sharply polarized between those in favor of a strong central government—centralists—and those in favor of a confederation of individual provinces—federalists. Caldas, meanwhile, was more interested in the daily operation of the Observatory and in a projected new career as a publisher. Abruptly he found himself obliged to join the centralist army as a military engineer. Having been forced to take a political stance, he soon repudiated the centralist government and joined the federalist cause. The ensuing civil war brought defeat to the federalists and chaos to Caldas.

There was temporary refuge to be found in the province of Antioquia. Here Caldas settled comfortably into the role of military engineer—building fortresses, overseeing the production of munitions and organizing a school for engineering cadets. But in Spain the French invasion had come to an end and the reconquest of America was set in motion.

The tempest of revolution had abruptly shattered the peacefulness of Caldas's scientific endeavors. Time and again Caldas tried to right himself in the maelstrom's wake. But its fury grew unabated until he was finally swept away.

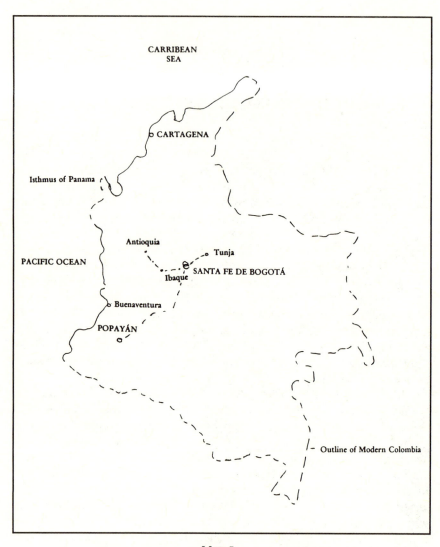

CARRIBEAN
SEA

○ CARTAGENA

Isthmus of Panama

PACIFIC OCEAN

Antioquia

Tunja

Ibaque

SANTA FE DE BOGOTÁ

○ Buenaventura

POPAYÁN
○

Outline of Modern Colombia

MAP 5.

Lost in the Revolutionary Maelstrom: 1810–1816.

– – – The Federalist Revolt. 1812. Bogota – Tunja – Bogota.

·–·– Escape to Antioquia. 1813. Return to Bogota. 1815.

– – – Escape to Popayán. 1816. March to Death. Popayán – Bogota. 1816.

X. THE DAWN OF INDEPENDENCE

Francisco José de Caldas's life had a number of strikingly clear turning points. First, as he traveled amidst the natural beauty of the Andes, working as an itinerant merchant, Caldas decisively determined to pursue the study of science. For several years, a scientist in search of community, he did the best he could working with what was at hand. When he joined the Botanical Expedition, Caldas became part of institutionalized science and developed an original program of investigation. As director of the Astronomical Observatory, he furthered his work with great intensity in astronomy, geography and botany, in addition to establishing the *Semanario*. He had reached a position of leadership in the scientific community.

All of these turning points were positive. Caldas grew from an isolated amateur to a competent professional, from a lawyer turned merchant to a scientist, from a provincial unknown to a national leader. Given the economic and political limitations on the growth of science in Nueva Granada, Caldas had done amazingly well. Following Mutis's death and the subsequent reorganization of the expedition, Caldas looked forward to a period of economic and professional stability.

It is chilling to note, then, that the final turning point in Caldas's life — the independence of Nueva Granada — should so completely and effectively undo his plans for the future. It is unnerving to realize that the life of an individual can be so mercilessly overcome by events beyond his control.

PRELUDE TO INDEPENDENCE

It was Caldas's generation that took the first steps on the long and tortuous road to independence. An avid reader and correspondent, he was well aware of the events that were to lead to the overthrow of Spanish authority. The first manifestation by Caldas's generation of nationalist sentiment came in 1794. Antonio Nariño, a well educated, well-to-do Creole, translated from French to Spanish the "Declaration of the Rights of Man and Citizen" written by the French National Assembly five years earlier. Since Nariño was Treasurer of the Viceroyalty and friend to Viceroy Ezpletia, he was able to print it without prior approval. The publication circulated only among Nariño's circle of friends. Concurrently, bills were furtively posted in the streets of Bogotá mocking the colonial government. Viceroy Ezpletia, who had been away from Bogotá, ordered prosecution of the wrongdoers. Spanish officials were preoccupied with the infiltration of foreign literature and anxious to suppress any challenge to royal authority.

The judicial process that followed was intended not so much to punish the publication of revolutionary literature, as to discredit and dismantle the network of young Creole intellectuals who carried out the deed. Nariño was an energetic and charismatic figure well-known in the capital of the viceroyalty. Caldas probably became acquainted with Nariño while a law student in Bogotá, but was not one of Nariño's "followers." The judgment of the court was that Nariño should be sent to one of Spain's African prisons and be condemned to lifelong exile. Along with Nariño, prison terms were given to Francisco Antonio Zea, second-in-command in the Botanical Expedition, and Sinforoso Mutis, among other "conspirators." The adventurous Nariño managed to jump ship upon arrival in Spain. Following his escape he traveled through Europe focusing his attention on events in France. Finally he returned to Nueva Granada and subjected himself to the control of local authorities. The other conspirators were eventually acquitted by Spanish courts—a clear rebuke to the arbitrary proceedings of the colonial government.

At the time of this scandal, Caldas wandered quietly through the Andes working as an itinerant merchant and opening his eyes to the possibility of doing science in Spanish America. His comment on the affair shows that his mind was not on politics, "Yes, I am concerned for this capital [Bogotá] with the extraordinary and crazy conduct of Nariño. It is our fortune, though without merit, to enjoy in these surroundings an unalterable tranquility, in the midst of the greatest revolutions of the universe."[1]

It was no coincidence that members of the Botanical Expedition (Sinforoso Mutis and Francisco Antonio Zea) were to be found in the ranks of the early movement for independence. The labor of José Celestino Mutis had profoundly affected the citizenry of Nueva Granada and it may well be argued that the elder Mutis had directed the enlightenment of an entire generation. Certainly Mutis was no revolutionary; he did not espouse the separation of the American colonies from Spain. But he had brought to the Granadians two notions that were fundamental to the growth of nationalist sentiment.

First, Mutis taught scientific reasoning. A world-class scholar, he dealt naturally with scientific concepts despite the possibility of coming into conflict with the intellectual oppression practiced by the Spanish government and the Catholic Church. It is curious, indeed, that Mutis, a priest, was accused of heresy for teaching Copernicanism, with which the Vatican had long since come to terms. The influence of ultraconservative clergy and obedient monarchists in Nueva Granada continued to play an important role as the eighteenth century came to an end. Mutis contributed a new mode of thought, one which would eventually undercut Spanish authority, by his example as director of the Botanical Expedition; through his correspondence; as a teacher; and by his activist expansion of science in the colony, including the construction of the Observatory.

---

[1] Eduardo Posada, ed. *Cartas de Caldas*. Biblioteca de Historia Nacional. Volume 15. Imprenta Nacional. Bogotá. 1917, p. 2.

Second, Mutis brought national pride to the Granadians in a way that no other person could. He pointed out the importance of the rich local flora and urged the inhabitants to know their surroundings. He aided in the establishment of a "Society of Friends of the Nation," which intended to promote local development. Mutis understood, of course, the nascent nationalism to be one within the body of the Spanish Empire, but he planted the idea which later bore fruit in the hands of his students.

The revolution of 1810 found its greatest support among the young intellectuals who were members, friends or in some other way associated with the circle centered about the expedition. Caldas, too, was part of this group. It should be remembered, though, that he arrived in Bogotá only at the end of 1805, isolated until then in the Ecuadorean Andes, far from the intense debates of the capital which nurtured the desire for independence. Furthermore, Caldas was not a firebrand. Rather, he tended to be conservative and reserved in his personal conduct, displaying passion only for his work as a scientist. Thus, as events led inexorably toward revolution, Caldas maintained a moderate stance, looking for stability, not a break with the past.

In Europe, Napoleon Bonaparte was strengthening the military and political power of France, at a time when the Spanish monarchy was suffering a decline in its ability to govern. Taking advantage of internal disputes between Spain's King Carlos IV and the heir to the throne, Fernando, Napoleon seized power in May 1808. Two months later Napoleon's brother, Joseph, became King of Spain. In the face of the capitulation of the monarchy and the French invasion, a Supreme Junta was formed which pretended not only to represent the Spanish people but also to continue to govern the Spanish American colonies. In Nueva Granada Viceroy Amar found support for proclaiming Fernando VII as rightful monarch, declaring war against France and sending financial aid to the Supreme Junta.

In January 1809 the Junta declared the colonies to be an integral part of Spain and offered to seat representatives sent from America. The offer, however, did not give the colonies any real power and thus did not meet with enthusiasm. There was a general feeling that Nueva Granada should be an integral part of the Spanish Empire, but with rights equal to Spain. In November Camilo Torres, Caldas's cousin, wrote a "Memorandum of Offenses" (*Memorial de Agravios*) in which he denounced the injustices of Spanish rule. Thus as the situation in Spain disintegrated, Creole revolutionaries began to sense that their opportunity had arrived.

Caldas apparently did not believe the situation to be so critical. In March 1810 he directed a letter to Antonio Narvaez who had been named to represent Nueva Granada in the Supreme Junta. Caldas accompanied the letter with copies of his *Semanario*. He petitioned Narvaez to seek official approval of the Observatory and his own position. Thus, four months prior to the upheaval in Bogotá, Caldas was looking to Spain for support. Indeed, Caldas appears to have maintained cordial relations with Viceroy Amar up until the July revolution.

This is not to say that Caldas was a royalist. Quite to the contrary, he was a patriot in the most fundamental sense of the term. For Caldas knew his nation—his "patria"—as no other Creole knew it. He had meticulously measured its geography, collected its flora and written of possible improvements to its commerce. When Caldas spoke in favor of Nueva Granada he did so with details and data, not just sentiment. Caldas was firmly bound to his land. He had not traveled to Europe as had many of his contemporaries. Following the momentary illusion of traveling with Humboldt, Caldas realized that his future lay in America. As he was profoundly dedicated to the scientific study of the "patria," however, so was he averse to taking action which could interrupt his work. Certainly Caldas was more of a scientist than a revolutionary, but he was as much a patriot as any person in Nueva Granada.

CALDAS TAKES A WIFE

The story of Caldas's marriage helps to shed some light on his personality and gives a better understanding of the forces that motivated him during the troubled times to come.

As one reads Caldas's letters and writings there is a distinct lack of references to women other than his own relatives or his friends' wives. He often gave the impression that he was a seminarian. Certainly part of his empathy with José Celestino Mutis may have come from Mutis's vocation as a priest. Both Mutis and Caldas placed emphasis on the study of science at the expense of an interest in "worldly" affairs. Part of the coolness in Caldas's relationship with Humboldt was a result of the baron's enjoyment of the social life in Quito. Caldas felt that Humboldt, whom he greatly admired, was acting out of character for a man of science. In a very straightforward manner Caldas described himself as ". . . a man who looked upon the women of the Earth with cold indifference . . . a man submerged among books, instruments, with his eyes fixed upon the sky. . . ."[2]

It comes as a surprise, then, when in early 1810 Caldas began his correspondence with his future wife. Why did he suddenly take an interest in marriage? How did a man with "cold indifference" for women so quickly find a bride? One can only speculate. Caldas had shown before mercurial changes of temperament and an ability to bring intensity to a cause quickly once convinced that he should do so. I find the only possible explanation is that in 1809, following the resolution of Mutis's testament, Caldas finally came to enjoy economic and professional stability. It seems likely then that the fortyish Caldas reasoned it was time he searched for a mate. And so he did.

The mechanics of making the match were really quite simple. Caldas wrote to his friends in Popayán, asking them to find a potential wife. This

---

[2] Jorge Arias de Greiff, et al., eds. *Cartas de Caldas*. Academia Colombiana de Ciencias Exactas, Fisicas y Naturales. Bogotá. 1978, p. 302.

probably occurred in the latter half of 1809. One of Caldas's friends, Agustin Barahona, did indeed have a candidate, his niece Manuela, who was under his care. So the problem was neatly resolved and by 1810 the marriage of Francisco José de Caldas and Manuela Barahona had already been arranged.

Without ever having met Manuela ("I confess. . . . that five months ago I was unaware of your existence,"[3]) Caldas assumed the role of romantic suitor with the intensity he had earlier shown for astronomy, geography and botany. He sent Manuela silk gloves and rings of emeralds, rubies and diamonds. He asked for her shoe size so that he might present her well-dressed to Viceroy Amar. In addition, Caldas began to search for a house, for he had to leave the first floor of the Observatory which was his home as a bachelor.

There is little information available on the bride-to-be. Manuela was about twenty years younger than Caldas. Permission had to be obtained from the Church for the marriage because she was a distant relative of Caldas. In the letter seeking the Church's permission Caldas wrote:

The girl I pretend [to marry] is poor and obscure in Popayán. Her parents, so that she might receive a Christian education have given custody to an aunt who has generously raised her. In addition, I have been informed that she is between 19 and 20 years of age and runs the risk, owing to her poverty, and the abundance of women and shortage of men in Popayán, of not accommodating herself in an honest marriage as I pretend.[4]

Caldas apparently had thought of what to expect in a wife. He wrote to his friend Santiago Arroyo, "I have sought neither beauty nor riches; virtue, birth, will suffice for a well-formed heart."[5]

But what did Manuela think of this? Caldas had not been in Popayán since 1805. She may have seen him then through the eyes of an adolescent. Now Caldas was well-known and well-established. Manuela had spent the intervening years in her uncle's house because her own parents were unable to care for her. Caldas had traveled throughout the viceroyalty; Manuela had probably never left Popayán. She asked Caldas to allow her to take along to Bogotá a younger brother. Caldas politely demurred. In any case, she may have had no better alternative.

On 13 May 1810 the marriage ceremony was performed in Popayán. Caldas, however, was in Bogotá. His friend, Antonio Arboleda, served as his representative. From the moment it occurred to Caldas that he should marry until some four months following the ceremony, Caldas did not know his wife. In mid-June Manuela was sent from Popayán on the long and difficult journey through semi-tropical valleys and cold mountain trails to meet the astronomer who had become her husband.

There is no way to judge the happiness of Caldas's marriage, but it

---

[3] Ibid., 301.
[4] Ibid., 303.
[5] Ibid., 307.

is certain that he and his Manuela had to endure many hardships. They had four children, the first two of whom died in infancy. During the six and one-half years from their marriage until Caldas's death they were separated at least two years. In fact, he never knew his second child who died at one month of age, nor his fourth child who was born shortly before his own execution. The revolution was hard on the couple. Manuela was, for a short time, put under house arrest. Their possessions were embargoed. They had to flee Bogotá in difficult circumstances. Through it all Caldas treated Manuela with, at least, paternal affection, lecturing her often in his letters on how to lead a Christian life. His family brought Caldas both preoccupations and stability during the tempest that swelled about them as the Granadians sought independence from Spain.

Revolutionary Fervor

By mid-year 1810 Spain was no longer in a position to control events in Nueva Granada. The interim Supreme Junta claimed authority over American affairs but had to appeal to the colonies' willingness to remain in the Empire, for the Junta lacked the power to enforce its wishes. The Creoles were confronted with the problem of how to react to a weakened Spain. If independence was the objective, what were the steps to be taken?

It has been suggested[6] that the intellectual leaders of the movement for independence met in the Observatory to discuss plans of action. It is reasonable to assume that, in fact, the future leaders of the revolution could be found in the evenings in Caldas's apartment on the first floor of the Observatory. They were, after all, members of the Botanical Expedition, friends and relatives of Caldas. In his correspondence Caldas gives ample evidence that his acquaintances would come to visit.

But if there were discussion groups, most likely they dealt with the general problem of Spanish oppression. Caldas could be expected to complain about Spanish control of books and other literature; the poor educational system; about American isolation from Europe; and about the need for more support for science. Certainly he, like his colleagues, resented the exclusion of Creoles from decision making and the blatant discrimination practiced by Spaniards against the supposedly second-class Creoles. However, if there were detailed plans for an uprising against the colonial government, if the visitors to the Observatory— Lozano, Mutis, Pombo, Torres—were acting as conspirators, then I believe that it must be concluded that Caldas was absent from these discussions. Perhaps he tired of the conversation and chose to work on his manuscripts or his plant collections. Or perhaps he would climb to the dome and search for stars through Bogotá's murky night sky.

There is no indication that Caldas was prepared for the actual break

---

6 Enrique Perez Arbelaez. *José Celestino Mutis y la Real Expedición Botánica del Nuevo Reyno de Granada*. Instituto Colombiano de Cultura Hispánica. Bogotá. 1983, p. 189.

with Spain. He was preoccupied with arranging quarters for Manuela's arrival; he continued to publish the *Semanario*; and on 16 July 1810 he wrote his reply to a brochure published by the priest and former expedition member Eloy Valenzuela (see Chapter IX). For Caldas, business continued as usual.

Meanwhile, the tension between Spanish expectations and Granadian reality had come to the breaking point. At the end of May 1810 representatives from the Spanish regency council for America had arrived in the colony. Their mission was to enlist the solidarity of the colonies in the struggle against France. But the Creoles would have none of it. As the representatives traveled inland, uprisings against the authority of the Regency Council occurred in Cartagena, Pamplona and Socorro. On 20 July 1810 the Council representatives were expected in Bogotá and a banquet was to be held in their honor.

The Twentieth of July happened to be market day. When a group of Creoles went to buy a flower pot to put at the banquet table, the shop owner, a Spaniard, derided them with insults. Voices were raised, fists began to fly, crowds gathered and suddenly the storm was unleashed.

The mob gained strength. Confronted by the reality of Spain's weakness, the city edged dangerously toward anarchy; however, the intellectuals who had encouraged the sentiment for independence managed to gain control. A Supreme Junta was named which included, among others, Caldas's cousin—Camilo Torres, Caldas's friend—Miguel Pombo and Caldas's colleague—Sinforoso Mutis. The Junta took action to assert Granadian control of the government. Viceroy Amar was taken prisoner on 25 July, removed from Bogotá on 15 August and deported to Cuba from Cartagena on 12 October. The militia wavered momentarily but finally submitted to the authority of the Junta. The many royalists who remained in Bogotá apparently found it prudent to maintain a low profile and wait for future developments.

Caldas's comment on the uprising can be found in a letter written on 6 August to Manuela who was still on the trail, still waiting to meet her husband, "By now you must know of the terrible revolution that has occurred in the government. I was not injured, thank the Lord. . . ."[7] This comment seems sufficient evidence that Caldas was an observer, and not a protagonist, in the revolution of 20 July 1810.

Although Caldas termed the revolution "terrible," it is worth noting that it did not constitute a complete break with Spain. Rather, the Creoles carefully limited their aspirations. The revolution of 20 July did not seek complete independence from Spain. The Granadians still offered obedience to King Fernando, but that obedience was cleverly stipulated to depend on the king's arrival in Nueva Granada to exercise his power. The Granadians did reject the claims of the interim Spanish government.

---

[7] Jorge Arias de Greiff, et al., eds. *Cartas de Caldas*. Academia Colombiana de Ciencias Exactas, Fisicas y Naturales. Bogotá. 1978, p. 315.

They argued that the French invasion of Spain had brought about an abnormal situation which effectively abrogated the normal relation between Spain and the colonies. What they sought, at least for the moment, was control of their own regional government.

We must also note that the revolution of July 20 was limited to Bogotá. There was no coherent action throughout the viceroyalty although Bogotá's being the capital gave the event special importance. Movements similar to that in Bogotá sprang up in most, but not all, of the provinces. This lack of coordination and the inability to agree on a unified plan of action turned out to be fatal flaws for the Creoles' hopes.

If Caldas was initially overcome by events, he soon turned his energies to the cause of the new government. The Supreme Junta in Bogotá gave its permission for Caldas and an associate, Joaquin Camacho, to publish a political periodical. The Junta also loaned the sum of two thousand pesos for expenses, with payback scheduled some six months later. Thus on 27 August the *Diario Politico* was born. This was a record of political events, unlike the scientifically oriented *Semanario*. It was published three times weekly and lasted for forty-six issues, until near the end of 1810.

Caldas here had the opportunity to demonstrate his abilities as a writer, editor and publisher. He wrote, not of the geography of Nueva Granada, but of the cruelty and oppression of Spanish rule. The rapid demise of the *Diario Politico* was probably strictly a matter of economics.

The final memoir of the *Semanario*, written in March 1811, also dealt with news of the revolution—a deviation from its usual philosophy. In the midst of the agitation brought on by the revolution the publication of a scientific periodical probably became hopelessly utopic. When the *Diario Politico* could no longer be sustained, it seems likely that Caldas tried to reorient his *Semanario* to meet the public interest. This, too, came to no avail and Caldas's career as a publisher came to a momentary halt.

THE END OF THE EXPEDITION

Caldas's main preoccupation following the break with Spain was exactly what would become of his own position. He had made a great effort to gain the favor of Viceroy Amar in support of the Observatory. He was, until the last possible moment, active in seeking an official appointment from the Spanish government. Suddenly Caldas found himself afloat in a sea of uncertainty. He wrote to Manuela, "Now the matter is reform in the Observatory and the expedition; now the matter is my advancement or my ruin."[8]

Indeed, the end of Spanish rule brought with it an end to the formal organization of the expedition. The botanist and biographer of Mutis, Father Perez Arbelaez, wrote, "With the elimination of the representa-

---

[8] Ibid., 315.

tives of the King, the Royal Botanical Expedition of the New Kingdom [of Granada] also comes to an end as a unified body."[9]

The new government in Bogotá had more pressing matters to deal with. Apparently Caldas was to some degree supported in running the Observatory. He did what he could to keep the Observatory operating, just as Sinforoso Mutis continued to work on the collections of the expedition and Salvador Rizo tried to keep the expedition's painters at their drawing tables. As the new provincial governments groped for a sense of direction, the scientific enterprise in Nueva Granada was inexorably reduced to the efforts of individuals amidst the exhilaration and confusion brought by revolution.

---

[9] Enrique Perez Arbelaez. *José Celestino Mutis y la Real Expedición Botánica del Nuevo Reyno de Granada*. Instituto Colombiano de Cultura Hispánica. Bogotá. 1983, p. 189.

XI. THE CLOUDS OF CIVIL WAR

The overthrow of Spanish authority in Nueva Granada proceeded with relative ease. There had been no resistance of consequence from royalist forces and the Creoles understood that Spain was incapable of waging war for the moment. Independent governments proliferated in the provincial capitals and secondary cities throughout the former viceroyalty. By the end of 1810 only Panama and Rioacha to the north and Popayán, Pasto and Quito to the south remained under royalist control. In early 1811 the new governments flexed their muscles. Counterrevolutionary movement in Cartagena was suppressed. Troops from Bogotá, under the orders of Colonel Antonio Baraya, were sent to oust royalists in the south. A stunning victory by Baraya freed Popayán. There was every reason for the Granadians to applaud their own success. The dawn of independence brought an apparent calm under which a new nation could be built.

Had Spain not suffered the intrigues of Napoleon, the uprisings in Nueva Granada would have been unthinkable. At the very least, the Granadians would have had to create a unified front in order to remove the colonial yoke. As it was, however, the inability of Spain to enforce its control permitted the success of a series of uncoordinated but simultaneous provincial revolutions. Thus the Granadians' success in removing Spanish authority left them, at the same time, facing the dilemma of self-government. While they were sure that they did not want to continue as subjects of a colonial government, there was no consensus as to just what form of political organization should be instituted.

Opinion became polarized around two alternatives, centralism vs. federalism. The centralists supported a strong central government. They argued that the independent provinces should seek strength through unity and that centralism would provide the order necessary to defend the new nation from an eventual Spanish threat. On the other hand, the federalists wanted to create a union of equal independent provinces. For the federalists, the struggle against the excesses of authoritarian Spanish colonialism should not lead to the establishment of a new, authoritarian centralist government.

Despite the philosophical differences, the opposing forces basically reflected geographical prejudices. Centralism was supported by Bogotá, which had been the capital of the viceroyalty and which expected to continue to exercise its predominance. The federalists tended to have their roots in the provinces. As such, they rejected the idea of subjecting themselves to Bogotá. Caldas's first biographer, Lino de Pombo, succinctly described the situation, "Each province wanted to be a sovereign state and if they had something in common it was hatred of Bogotá."[1]

Caldas was not active in the formulation of political alternatives, but his natural place was with the federalist cause. A native of Popayán, he had come to study and work in Bogotá as had many other provincials. They tended to conserve their regional identities. For example, Caldas's cousin, Camilo Torres was an idealogue for the federalists; and Caldas's friend, Miguel Pombo (also from Popayán) wrote a pamphlet espousing federalist ideals.

It is worth noting that Pombo translated the constitution of the United States of America into Spanish, the federalists claim to have been inspired by the U.S. model. Their interpretation of federalism in the United States was incorrect, however, as they supported a form of government closer to the notion of a "confederation" or the dominance of states' rights than to the federalism of the U.S. constitution of 1787 in which the central government's prerogative was predominant. Nevertheless, the terms centralism and federalism came to describe two opposing schools of thought which in reality pitted Bogotá against the rest of the provinces.

While the provinces debated the question of centralism vs. federalism, they each separately took up the task of organizing their own governments. Bogotá and its surrounding territory established the State of Cundinamarca in March 1811. Its constitution, written by Caldas's colleague in the Botanical Expedition, Jorge Tadeo Lozano, professed the Catholic faith and acknowledged the authority of Fernando VII as king (but did not recognize the authority of his delegates, i.e., the Viceroy). Lozano was elected the first president of Cundinamarca, but he did not enjoy much success and was forced to resign in September 1811 after less than six months in office—to be replaced by the charismatic Antonio Nariño who was a convinced centralist. Although Nariño had ample support in Cundinamarca, his personality exacerbated the suspicions of the federalists.

As the centralist position was gaining strength in Cundinamarca, the other provinces moved to establish a federalist government. Under the leadership of Camilo Torres a congress was called to discuss an Act of Confederation. The result was the formation of a Congress of the United Provinces of Nueva Granada in November 1811. The confederation was designed according to the federalist conception of equal and independent states. Only five of the provinces signed the act, but the confederation was nonetheless a major political counterweight to centralist Cundinamarca.

THE PERSISTENT ASTRONOMER

In the aftermath of the July revolution, Caldas, caught up in the uncertainty and confusion that affected the populace in general, was forced

---

[1] Lino de Pombo. "Francisco José de Caldas, Biografía del Sabio." In *Francisco José de Caldas.* Suplemento de la Revista de la Academia Colombiana de Ciencias Exactas, Fisicas y Naturales. Libreria Voluntad. Bogotá. 1958, p. 39.

to come to terms with a new state of affairs. He took up the cause of independence—as director of the *Diario Politico*—at the expense of his work in the Observatory and the consummation of his marriage. His young bride, Manuela, patiently continued her journey toward Bogotá as Caldas was repeatedly forced to delay his promise that he would meet her on the trail. By mid-September, though, a certain calm had set in and Caldas was able to leave Bogotá and meet his wife, at last. They must have returned quickly to the city since Caldas was responsible for two periodicals, *Diario Politico* and the *Semanario*, director of the Observatory, professor of mathematics and, I think it is reasonable to assume, an active member of a Botanical Expedition that had fallen into jurisdictional limbo.

The initial burst of revolutionary fervor carried Caldas along, but by the end of 1810 it had begun to lag. The *Diario Politico* came to a sudden end. Caldas tried to keep the *Semanario* alive by publishing a eulogy to a friend of his, Miguel Cabal, who had lost his life during the liberation of Popayán. Neither science nor politics, however, could capture sufficient readers. The *Semanario* had to be put to rest for lack of "a printing press and subscriptions."[2] A letter Caldas sent to Salvador Rizo in January 1811 indicates that the expedition was still functioning. In March, however, when former Expedition member Jorge Tadeo Lozano assumed the presidency of Cundinamarca he had to confront economic realities and did not seek continued support for the Expedition. Caldas was irate with his former colleague and friend, calling Lozano "a barbaric President."[3] Caldas further accused Lozano of having "nearly ruined the Observatory and Botanical Expedition."[4]

Clearly Caldas understood the implications of independence from Spain on his own situation. The new provincial government was unlikely to be able to assure support for the scientists, so Caldas began to look for means to support himself. In an edition of the *Semanario* in November 1810 he announced the publication of an almanac for the year 1811. In his preliminary announcement Caldas presented some of his own work in the fields of meteorology, geology and astronomy. He included a somewhat detailed discussion of the measurement of longitude using the moons of Jupiter. It seems that in addition to selling almanacs, Caldas was also trying to attract prospective students and collaborators as a means of maintaining support for the Observatory.

Caldas also published an almanac for the year 1812. In that one he widened his horizons, adding dates on ecclesiastical history, secular history and the history of science. He continued to espouse knowledge of astronomy and presented a discussion of terms such as syzygy, apogee, perigee and ecliptic. Furthermore, Caldas took the lead in calling for the

[2] Jorge Arias de Greiff, et al., eds. *Cartas de Caldas*. Academia Colombiana de Ciencias Exactas, Fisicas y Naturales. Bogotá. 1978, p. 317.
[3] Ibid., 317.
[4] Ibid., 317.

development of an independent science, "If we have shaken off the political yoke of Europe, let us also shake off that scientific dependence that
degrades us and that maintains us in a literary infancy more ignominious
than slavery."[5]

Caldas struggled to keep himself active as a scientist. He tried to promote public and private support for the Observatory, but in order to support himself and his family, he planned to establish his own printing
shop. To that end Caldas imported a printing press from the United
States. (It is worth noting the improvement in Caldas's financial situation
following the death of Mutis. That he could import a press attests to the
comfortable situation he enjoyed during the final year of Spanish rule.)
He hoped to publish for profit, and not limit his project to scientific materials. One of his associates, Benedicto Dominguez, was a former student
and later occupied the post of director of the Observatory.

During the end of 1810, all of 1811, and the beginning of 1812 Caldas
pressed on with his scientific work. He was interested in political developments, but they were of secondary importance to him. Instead he
emphasized the development of programs he had already begun in the
Expedition, in the Observatory and as a publisher. He also seems to have
settled comfortably into the role of a family man. His first child, a boy
named Liborio, was born in July 1811. Despite the limitations of the local
economy, Caldas managed to keep himself afloat and could feel somewhat hopeful for the future. There were internal and external conflicts,
however, that had yet to be resolved and hovered ominously above the
Granadians. In announcing Liborio's birth Caldas described him as, ". . . an
astronomical sprout, heir to the quadrant and telescope, and now to the
cannon and mortar as well."[6]

TAKING UP ARMS

The process of independence in Nueva Granada reached a critical junc-
ture at the end of 1811. In November the province of Cartagena declared
its absolute independence from Spain, thus ending any pretense of obedience to Fernando VII. The federalist United Provinces approved a constitution on 27 November. The isolation of the provinces came to an end,
and the first outline of a new nation took form. At the same time Spain
made its first response, albeit a feeble one, by naming a new viceroy in
March 1812. Without the support necessary to enforce his rule, the
viceroy came and went in six months finding haven only in the province
of Panama.

Although the Granadians became bolder in their position against
Spain, their internal conflicts also grew markedly. The consolidation of

---

[5] *Obras Completas de Francisco José de Caldas.* Universidad Nacional de Colombia.
Imprenta Nacional. Bogotá. 1966, p. 13.
[6] Jorge Arias de Greiff, et al., eds. *Cartas de Caldas.* Academia Colombiana de Ciencias
Exactas, Fisicas y Naturales. Bogotá. 1978, p. 317.

the federalist Congress was viewed as a threat by Cundinamarca's president, Antonio Nariño. When the Congress was installed in the city of Tunja, northeast of Bogotá, Nariño decided to send troops to the area under the pretext of preparing a defense against possible royalist attacks. Behind Nariño's justifications lay his real intentions—to force the neighboring provinces to join the state of Cundinamarca and the Congress to submit to centralist leadership.

The centralist army left Bogotá in early 1812 under the command of Colonel Antonio Baraya who months earlier had successfully ousted royalist forces from Popayán. Along with Baraya traveled a corps of engineers. Its director was Captain Francisco José de Caldas.

What combination of forces could have taken Caldas from his family, his Observatory and his newly acquired printing press to join in the centralist crusade? There is no clear account of this period in Caldas's letters, but he probably took at face value Nariño's assertion that this campaign was directed against probable royalist attacks. Moreover, Caldas was still receiving some support from the state of Cundinamarca, and he was thus an employee of Nariño. Caldas does mention that he took up the study of military matters as early as August 1811. Finally, Caldas probably felt that it was his patriotic obligation to join the campaign even though he was not inclined to the military life.

It is not certain just what engineering there was to be done. Most likely Caldas was commissioned to make reliable maps of the routes to be followed. In any case, he took time to observe his surroundings, just as he had done in his earlier travels near Bogotá, Popayán and Quito. Caldas had not seen this region before. So he planned to organize his observations—plant life, latitudes, longitudes, altitudes, distances, temperatures, barometric pressures—in a memoir that was to be one of the first publications of his press. Though civil war was almost inevitable, Caldas still managed to isolate himself in order to pursue his scientific work. He wrote from Tunja, "But, in the midst of the crisis I observe, calculate and draw, and only the current of politics makes me comment on things other than geography and astronomy."[7]

The military campaign against the federalist Congress never began. Coronel Baraya was apparently doubtful of the wisdom of taking an unborn nation into the throes of civil war. The troops remained immobile nearby while the military leadership debated what course of action to follow.

At the same time, Caldas abandoned his ambivalence with regard to the political future. He forthrightly joined the cause of the federalists and became an outspoken enemy of Antonio Nariño. It was clear to all that Nariño intended to unite the provinces by force under his own leadership. Caldas was incensed, "For more than a month we have been quartered

---

[7] Ibid., 327.

in this city [Tunja] because of the ambitious intrigues of Nariño, who only wants to divide and rule."[8]

Calling Nariño "a tyrant in disguise,"[9] Caldas made amends with his colleagues who supported the Congress. In Caldas's judgment Nariño was a dictator ". . . who called himself free and humane, and in 1794 published the Rights of Man, only to scandalously violate them in 1812."[10]

Caldas excused himself with Camilo Torres noting that he had erred in accepting a role in the centralist campaign, "I did not know the path I had taken . . ."[11] and by the end of April 1812 was a convinced federalist calling the Congress ". . . the last anchor we have in a tempest."[12]

Still, Caldas took a moderate attitude toward the political struggle. He thought it best to avoid factionalism and the mire of civil war. Along with many other Granadians Caldas felt that the new nation could ill afford to devote its limited resources to senseless warfare. He took it upon himself to convince his commander, Colonel Baraya, not to proceed against the Congress, "Every day we [Caldas and Baraya] spoke, and more than once I left my sextant to be able to convince the justly illustrious Baraya. . . ."[13]

While Baraya deliberated, his troops were transferred to nearby Sogamoso where they awaited orders. In Bogotá, Nariño became suspicious and sent for Baraya to return to the capital. But, Baraya pleaded for funds to be able to move the army, and continued to consider his options.

Some three months following his departure from Bogotá, Baraya made his decision and changed sides. On 25 May 1812 he issued the Proclamation of Sogamoso, which Caldas also signed, in which the authority of Antonio Nariño was disavowed. What had been a 10,000 man centralist army became a 10,000 man federalist army.

Nariño was not long in responding. A new contingent of troops was dispatched from Bogotá to bring the rebellious Baraya under control. Caldas, in the enemy camp, began to feel the pressure applied by Nariño. He had already asked friends to lend money to Manuela for his family's upkeep. The confrontation between Nariño and the Congress made both Caldas's family and his possessions target for reprisal. In June he wrote to Manuela "If it is necessary to hide yourself, then hide yourself along with my papers and books. Do not give the keys to the Observatory and say that I have them."[14]

To further complicate matters Manuela was expecting the couple's second child. This did not stop Nariño from putting her under arrest and attempting to embargo Caldas's printing press, furniture and scientific instruments. Caldas apparently could only rely on his associate, Bene-

8 Ibid., 324.
9 Ibid., 324.
10 Ibid., 330.
11 Ibid., 329.
12 Ibid., 327.
13 Ibid., 330.
14 Ibid., 332.

dicto Dominguez, to help them resolve these difficulties (even though Dominguez was a supporter of Nariño). Caldas received the support of Congress in demanding that Nariño free Manuela. Furthermore he wrote directly to Nariño, "You may afflict, intimidate and attack this innocent and virtuous girl; you may also do the same with my son and with all that is related to me in that wretched city [Bogotá]—nothing intimidates me."[15]

The expeditionary force from Bogota was forced to sign a truce with Baraya and return to the capital. The defeat forced Nariño to resign momentarily in August, but when Baraya decided to move his troops against Bogotá, Nariño reassumed power, this time as dictator. Meanwhile, Manuela gave birth to a daughter, Ignacia, who died before she was a month old. Caldas never knew her. He wrote to Manuela urging that she escape from Bogotá.

Congress, under the presidency of Camilo Torres, supported Baraya's plan to take the capital. In November, Nariño once again sent troops to halt the federalist advance and once again they were defeated. Thus by the end of 1812 the federalist forces were positioned for a victory. Nariño recognized that he was at a disadvantage and offered to negotiate a capitulation.

For a moment there was an opportunity to resolve the conflict between centralists and federalists peacefully, to find common cause and unite the nation for a battle against Spain that was sure to come. Inexplicably the moment was lost. Coronel Antonio Baraya, not content with Nariño's offer, wanted to take Bogotá by force. A meeting of the commanding officers was called. Caldas argued for the acceptance of Nariño's offer and voted against an attack, but, to no avail. Baraya was determined to conquer the capital and subjugate the centralists.

The inhabitants of Bogotá were in a hopeless situation. With nowhere else to turn they placed their faith in Nariño. On 9 January 1813 the final battle began. Baraya's troops were superior in number and should have won handily. But Nariño met the challenge with ingenuity. He sent a false message to one of Baraya's subordinates ordering that the federalist troops not be moved. The trick worked. With his back to the wall Nariño emerged victorious. The federalist troops were routed and dispersed.

Caldas was forced to flee with the rest of the federalist forces, while his family remained prisoner. The Observatory was beyond his grasp. He had been forced to take sides in the political dispute and had come agonizingly close to victory. But the prevalence of extremist positions led to the unnecessary spilling of Granadian blood. The peace and innocence of the scientist's isolation had come undone.

---

[15] Ibid., 336.

XII. DELUGE AND DARKNESS

Guilt and bitterness accompanied Caldas as he fled from Bogotá. Even though he had voted against the attack, the spilling of Granadian blood weighed heavily on his conscience. Caldas's response to the senseless fratricide was to look for a path which would allow him to escape from the maelstrom. He took up temporary residence in the town of Cartago and petitioned Nariño to let Manuela leave Bogotá. To Manuela he wrote of plans to travel together to Cartagena to find a ship that would take them elsewhere. Caldas sought refuge from a revolution that had lost its direction. He wrote to Manuela, "It is necessary, my child, to abandon this nation that cannot be free, and to seek asylum far from here where one neither sees crowns, nor hears the name of kings."[1]

Perhaps Caldas was correct and should have left Nueva Granada. Certainly that course of action was feasible in 1813. However, he did not have a clear destination, nor did he enjoy the economic solvency to take such a step. Another alternative was to return to his native Popayán, but on this account he complained bitterly about the lack of support from the federalist Congress, "Congress has forgotten me, they have not answered my letter nor have they given, for the money they owe me, a crumb of bread to my family; they have not given a recommendation for a position with the government of Popayán, and have disposed of my property without my being able to reply a single word."[2]

If Caldas was uncertain about his future he did not waver in his efforts to separate himself from the past. He had no wish to return to Bogotá, nor did he maintain any illusions about renewing his association with the Botanical Expedition or the Observatory. Caldas wrote to his associate, Benedicto Dominguez, announcing that "the Observatory has come to an end for me. . . ."[3]

He urged Dominguez to take charge of the Observatory and care for the instruments. So great were Caldas's feelings of deception and disgust that he retired from the most important position a scientist could find in Nueva Granada to seek some peace of mind. In addition, he gladly resigned his position as an engineer. Caldas eloquently summarized his attitude, and quite probably that of many other Granadians, "Now I am not an engineer, now I am not an official of the Union, I am simply F.J.

---

[1] Jorge Arias de Greiff, et al., eds. *Cartas de Caldas*. Academia Colombiana de Ciencias Exactas, Fisicas y Naturales. Bogotá. 1978, p. 344.

[2] Ibid., 344.

[3] Ibid., 344.

de Caldas and nothing more; with this mail I have sent my resignation and with four lines I have acquired my true necessities—my peace, my liberty, my mathematics and my tranquility."[4]

COLONEL CALDAS IN ANTIOQUIA

As Caldas considered the different possible routes he could follow, the movement for independence began to encounter elements of resistance. In Venezuela a royalist uprising had forced the retreat of Simón Bolivar whose tenacious leadership led the Granadians to independence years later. Bolivar arrived in Cartagena in November 1812. During the first months of 1813 he contributed to the liberation of communications along the Magdalena River and near the Venezuelan frontier. By May 1813 Bolivar had gained support for an expeditionary force to reconquer Venezuela.

To the South, the royalist stronghold of Quito supported an expedition of its own—this one directed Creole control in Pasto, Popayán and the Cauca River Valley. The invasion was successful and in May 1813 Popayán returned to royalist control. Caldas faced a dilemma. He could not return to Bogotá where Nariño was in firm control. The federalist Congress lacked authority and, in any case, he had broken his ties with the federalist movement. His logical destination, Popayán, was in royalist hands and his temporary residence, Cartago, lay in the intended path of the advancing royalist invasion.

Fortunately for Caldas an opportunity opened up for him in a region which heretofore he did not know—the province of Antioquia. From the beginnings of Granadian independence, Antioquia had followed a course of action somewhat separate from the rest of the provinces. Neither wholly federalist nor centralist, the government of Antioquia had avoided the debilitating effects of civil war. Faced with the royalist reconquest of the province of Popayán, Antioquia's neighbor to the south, a consensus was built around the naming of a dictator to deal with the extreme circumstances. Juan del Corral—twenty years Caldas's junior—assumed power in late July 1813. Del Corral is usually credited with calling Caldas to Antioquia. However, I find it reasonable to suppose that the idea came from one of Caldas's colleagues—perhaps José Manuel Restrepo who had collaborated in the *Semanario*, or Antonio Arboleda, Caldas's friend from Popayán who later held a position in the Antioquian government. Caldas had no other reasonable option. On 9 May 1813 he left Cartago hoping to find a safe haven in Antioquia.

The two and one-half years that Caldas spent as a military engineer at the service of the government of Antioquia are not as well documented as the rest of his life. Nonetheless it is possible to sketch the broad outlines of this period. Caldas worked as a military engineer, an employee

---

[4] Ibid., 344—footnote.

of the Antioquian government. He was given a variety of projects to complete, all of which were a challenge to his intellect. Considering the limitations under which he worked, Caldas demonstrated remarkable adaptability and ingenuity. Upon his initial experience as a military engineer in Bogotá, Caldas commented:

I am an engineer and for the defense of the nation I have had to seriously dedicate myself to the study of fortifications and artillery. It is true that these horrible sciences have their charm, but nothing of the majesty and grandeur of the skies. Fortunately, they are well-defined sciences so that two or three months of methodic study are enough to master them.[5]

Caldas's arrival in Antioquia coincided with the province's declaration of absolute independence from Spain, following the lead of Cartagena in November 1812 and Cundinamarca in July 1813, a month earlier than Antioquia. The most pressing problem for the Antioquians was defending themselves from a possible attack by the royalist forces that had taken control of Popayán and the Cauca River Valley to the south of Antioquia. Caldas was charged with the building of fortifications along the Cauca River. Until October 1813 Caldas worked in rustic conditions with the inhabitants of nearby villages to erect the stone fortresses with provisions for artillery, parapets and living quarters. He also set to work on a map of Antioquia's southern frontier for the purpose of military planning. The measurement of geographical positions had become a habit for Caldas and provided a link between his enjoyment of the pursuit of science and the stark necessity of preparing for war.

The position of the Republic of Antioquia with regard to the royalist advance was defensive. In Bogotá, however, the State of Cundinamarca, under Antonio Nariño, prepared an expeditionary force to oust the royalists from Popayán and assert the leadership the centralists felt belonged to them. Ironically, while Caldas labored with limited resources to defend against the nation's enemies, Nariño supplied his own engineers with equipment from the Observatory which was cared for by Benedicto Dominguez. The fiery Nariño headed south in September 1813. A brilliant campaign led to the liberation of Popayán in January 1814 and filled the centralists with enough confidence to pursue the enemy to the city of Pasto. But there, Nariño had overstepped his reach. The royalists regrouped amid a friendly citizenry while Nariño's troops lost discipline and coherence. The result was a shocking defeat for the Creoles in Pasto in May 1814. Nariño surrendered and was removed from the revolutionary scene. He had the fortune to be spared execution and was sent to prison in Spain.

While viewing the ebb and flow of conflict just beyond their borders, the Antioquians determined to bolster their own armed forces. Caldas fit into these plans as engineer general for a school of military engi-

---

[5] Ibid., 317.

neering cadets established in the city of Rionegro. The school was organized in early 1814 and the cadets began their studies in October. In an
inaugural speech, published in 1815, Caldas described the philosophy
and program of studies of the academy, which it would seem reasonable
to assume, were probably wholly of Caldas's making. He dealt extensively with the ethics that should guide a good soldier. He emphasized
the need for scientific knowledge and spoke to the students of the "lau-
rels, immortal glory and virtue. . . ."[6] that would be theirs for contributing to the defense of the nation. The speech was primarily a discourse
on morals in which Caldas listed military virtues—honor, courage, patience, obedience, reserve, zeal—in order to motivate a vibrant patriotism
in his charges.

The engineering program was appropriately well-organized and succinct. Mathematical subjects—arithmetic, geometry, trigonometry, algebra—
constituted the core materials. Six semesters were to be devoted to cover
the following special topics, one each semester: military architecture or
fortifications; artillery—the construction of rifles, cannon, etc.; military
geography, principally map-making; tactics; and civil engineering.
Caldas was able to carry out this program only until the end of 1815,
when he returned to Bogotá.

Caldas also took charge of the manufacture of war materials. A nitrate
mill was put in production in February 1815. Six months later a foundry
of rifle barrels was producing two units per day. He organized the casting
of artillery pieces and the production of gunpowder. In addition, Caldas
mounted the presses to establish the mint of the Republic of Antioquia.
These are indications of extraordinary activity on Caldas's part. Added
to this, he was reunited with his family and he enjoyed the financial support of the Antioquian government. It seemed that Caldas had indeed
found an island of tranquility in a sea of unrest.

Yet if armed conflict had not come to Antioquia, it was not far away.
The preparations for warfare were intense, as was the desire for freedom.
Caldas, in describing his own feelings wrote, ". . . this heart which con-
centrates the blackest and most implacable hatred against the Spanish
race, against this infamous, cruel, unjust and stupid nation."[7]

The Granadians in 1815 were still struggling for independence. However, they were not acting as a nation but as an incoherent group of repub-
lics. Nor were they struggling against Spain. By and large they were
fighting among themselves. For too long they had lived under the illusion that the revolution had already been won. If Caldas displayed a
staunch and energetic position in preparing for local royalist uprisings,
his efforts were in vain because the Granadians had failed to unite to
meet the real threat—the return of Spanish troops.

---

[6] *Obras Completas de Francisco José de Caldas.* Universidad Nacional de Colombia.
Imprenta Nacional. Bogotá. 1966, p. 56.

[7] Jorge Arias de Greiff, et al., eds. *Cartas de Caldas.* Academia Colombiana de Ciencias
Exactas, Fisicas y Naturales. Bogotá. 1978, p. 347.

The New Conquistadors

Events far from Nueva Granada were shaping the destiny of the intellectuals who took the first step toward independence. In Europe, the end
of French domination of Spain opened the possibility for a new balance
in the relationship between the "Madre Patria" and her American colonies. Fernando VII assumed the throne in May 1814 and in doing so dis-
pelled any doubts that his would be other than absolute rule. The opportunity to deal with the colonies on an equal basis was shunned and the
conquest of Spanish America began anew.

In Nueva Granada the royalist position gained strength while Fernando prepared an expeditionary force. The defeat of Nariño in Pasto left
Cundinamarca without a leader capable of advancing the centralist
cause. The provinces, federalist and centralist, were in disarray, each preparing its own defenses, as with Caldas's work in Antioquia. And, in September 1814, Simón Bolivar arrived again in Cartagena following his
defeat in Venezuela. Focusing on the need for unity Bolivar joined the
federalists in pressing Cundinamarca to join the Congress of the United
Provinces. When negotiations failed, Bolivar marched on Bogotá and
took the city in December 1814.

The attack on Bogotá marked a further setback for the moribund scientific community. With Caldas manufacturing arms in Antioquia and
Salvador Rizo a member of Bolivar's army, only Sinforoso Mutis remained
active among the triumvirate that inherited the Botanical Expedition of
José Celestino Mutis. The expedition was managed by a non-scientist,
Juan Jurado Lainez, from 1813 to 1815. In a report written in July 1815,
Jurado accused Rizo of robbing materials, Caldas of the theft of one thousand volumes from the expedition's library and denounced the lack of
inventories and general disorder. The veracity of this report is open to
question as Jurado was almost certainly an appointee of Nariño and may
have had a political axe to grind. But the accusation of disorder was probably accurate. The political upheaval, the exile of Caldas in Antioquia,
the confrontation between Salvador Rizo and Sinforoso Mutis, the use
of the Observatory equipment in Nariño's expedition to Popayán and the
confiscation of Caldas's possessions had inevitably weakened the expedition and the Observatory. So, when Bolivar's troops entered Bogota,
"looted and broke the best instruments"[8] of the Observatory, and were
stopped short of destroying the Expedition's herbaria by a frantic Sinforoso Mutis, it was another in a series of calamities that battered what
had once been a burgeoning scientific enterprise.

The federalists took charge of Bogotá in January 1815 and incorporated
Cundinamarca into the United Provinces. Faced with royalist forces to
the south in Popayán, and to the north in Panama, Santa Marta and
Rioacha, the new government supported Bolivar in the preparation of an

---

[8] Enrique Perez Arbelaez. *José Celestino Mutis y la Real Expedición Botánica del Nuevo
Reyno de Granada.* Instituto Colombiano de Cultura Hispánica. Bogotá. 1983, p. 193.

expeditionary force to attack Santa Marta. When Bolivar arrived at the Caribbean coast the government of Cartagena was unwilling to join him. Furthermore, the first contingent of Spanish forces reached Venezuela in April 1815. Bolivar prudently resigned his command and set sail for Jamaica in May—his opportune escape permitting him to organize and gain support for a final victorious campaign. But the liberation of South America from the Spanish Empire would come too late for Caldas.

Fernando VII chose as head of the expeditionary force General Pablo Morillo and equipped him with 11,000 troops including artillery, cavalry and a corps of engineers. Morillo, severe in temperament, was a neo-conquistador who came to Nueva Granada to subjugate rebellious colonials. He had no interest in seeking reconciliation. Morillo's chief of staff, Pascual Enrile, was an expert navigator and had been charged with recovering Spain's investment in the Botanical Expedition. The Spanish forces left Cadiz in early 1815, arrived in Venezuela in April and set siege to Cartagena in August.

The decision to force the surrender of Cartagena, the first province to declare its absolute independence from Spain, pitted the strength of the Spaniards against the zeal of the patriots. The port city was surrounded, its lines of communication, marine and terrestrial, were severed. In a heroic defense the citizenry staved off the invaders for more than three months. But, on 6 December 1815, victim of famine and pestilence, the city of Cartagena succumbed to Morillo's troops.

The irresistible force brought to bear on Cartagena signaled the Granadians that they were confronted with a militarily superior enemy. The spiritual effects of the fall of Cartagena were devastating. No longer were there calls for the nation's defense; rather there was hope for accommodation, for some type of arrangement.

In Bogotá, Caldas's cousin, Camilo Torres, was named president of the United Provinces (November 1815) and was authorized to negotiate peace with the Spanish forces. At this point Caldas reappeared in Bogotá, having fled from Antioquia which was under imminent danger of invasion. In what may be the best characterization of Caldas's years in Antioquia, it is noteworthy that the province capitulated to troops invading from the north, and that Caldas's fortresses, built on the southern frontier some two years earlier had proved useless. The federalist government, or perhaps Torres personally, called Caldas to Bogotá to complete his map of the nation and establish a school for military engineers, presumably similar to the one he directed in Antioquia. If Caldas really thought he might revive the Observatory and see printed an atlas of Nueva Granada it was because he, like many of his countrymen, were stunned as they tried to comprehend the cruelty with which the Spanish juggernaut advanced.

EL TERROR

General Morillo moved quickly following the capitulation of Cartagena. Dividing his army in four units, he directed them inland along the Cauca River, the Magdalena River and other main lines of communication. With his troops, Morillo sent promises of a pardon for those who would willingly surrender. For some Granadians this was a ray of hope, but most of the leadership recognized Morillo's offer for what it was—a cynical lie, for he planned to divide and conquer. The pardon was aimed at undermining support for continued resistance, while the real fate that awaited the most notable patriots was death.

Panic and dismay gripped Bogotá. The last vestiges of the new nation crumbled. Discussion centered around whether to escape to the tropical lowlands to the east, or to travel south toward Popayán where the Creoles had once again ousted the royalists some months earlier. Some decided to remain in the city and await clemency. Those who headed east eventually were joined by Bolivar and formed the nucleus of the army that finally won independence. Those that traveled south only prolonged their suffering.

For Caldas the first step in his viacrucis meant abandoning his family. In March 1816 Camilo Torres resigned the presidency. He and Caldas took the route to Popayán. In a village along the way Caldas wrote to Manuela with his final instructions, ". . . the farewell I gave you may be the last if we are subjugated by the Spaniards, because I am firmly resolved to abandon this nation which gave me birth before suffering the ridicule, prison and torture which our enemies have prepared for us."[9]

The situation was further complicated by the fact of Manuela's fourth pregnancy. Their first child, Liborio, had died while they were in Antioquia, but a daughter, Juliana, was born in the same period. Caldas entrusted the children's upbringing to his wife, "Take care my dear child; care for the education of Julianita and the child in your womb; teach them to fear God, and to be virtuous even though orphaned and poor. . . ."[10]

Manuela and the children went to live with an aunt. All of Caldas's possessions were at their disposition to pay his debts and provide for their necessities. In the desperation and anarchy that engulfed them, Caldas was only able to offer Manuela his feelings, "Keep me in your heart, love me, as I keep you in mine and will love you until death."[11]

Along with Torres and others, Caldas traveled toward Popayán in hope of a miracle. There was news from the port city of Buenaventura, on the Pacific coast, that an English buccaneer was anchored there, but this possibility of escape vanished quickly as the ship set sail before they arrived. Antioquia fell to the Spanish in April 1816 and Bogotá was taken in early May. Only Popayán remained free.

The entry of General Pablo Morillo into Bogotá marked the beginning of a period of terror for the Creoles. The promise of clemency was forgotten and Morillo quickly imprisoned the revolutionary leaders. It is not

---

[9] Jorge Arias de Greiff, et al., eds. *Cartas de Caldas.* Academia Colombiana de Ciencias Exactas, Fisicas y Naturales. Bogotá. 1978, p. 350.

[10] Ibid., 351.

[11] Ibid., 351.

possible to judge what news of Bogotá reached Caldas as he arrived in Popayán, or what his perception of Spanish intentions was. One wonders why he did not intern himself in the vast cordillera or in the dense jungle of the Pacific coast. Caldas was, after all, an experienced traveler and an expert geographer. He should have been able to elude the Spaniards indefinitely. Perhaps such a choice seemed useless. The momentum of the Spanish reconquest and the helter-skelter collapse of independent Nueva Granada may have made all alternatives appear equally dismal. Caldas chose instead to retreat to his family's hacienda, the same site where years earlier he had tested his hypsometric scale.

Then, the inevitable occurred. Royalist forces captured Popayán at the end of June 1816. Shortly thereafter, a patrol searching south of the city found Caldas and took him prisoner. He was taken back to the city and jailed while the local Spanish commander awaited orders from Bogotá. Caldas grasped at the only opportunity available to him—a plea for clemency. Fernando VII had offered to pardon those who voluntarily surrendered and submitted to the authority of the crown, with the condition that their conduct be reviewed. Along with two fellow prisoners Caldas wrote a letter on 21 July 1816 in which they repudiated the "delirium" of the revolution. The letter was not addressed to General Morillo in Bogotá, rather to the president of Quito, Toribio Montes. Apparently Montes had demonstrated decency in his treatment of the Granadians, since Caldas and his companions asked to be transferred to prison in Quito and kept under Montes's control.

Caldas was further afflicted when his mother died in his arms during a prison visit. She had sent her own letter to Montes with his pleading for her son's life. Although the situation grew increasingly difficult, there came a glimmer of hope when Montes acceded to the petitions of Caldas and his mother, and offered to transfer Caldas to Quito where he could live with one of his brothers. That offer must have taken on even more importance for Caldas when on 19 August a friend of his, José Maria Cabal, was executed in the public square of Popayán.

But that last means of escape was closed when General Morillo's orders were received demanding that the prisoners be sent to Bogotá. Caldas appealed to Montes to intercede on his behalf with Morillo. Yet when he left Popayán in early September he must have known that he had begun a long march to his death.

In the month-long trip from Popayán to Bogotá the pressure on Caldas was dreadful. His mother had died. He knew nothing of his wife and daughter. His scientific career was a distant memory. His involvement with the revolution had brought him imprisonment, not liberty. And the cruel, bloodthirsty General Morillo was efficiently eliminating a generation of Granadian intellectuals. By the time Caldas left he surely knew of the execution of Jorge Tadeo Lozano, who often visited Caldas in the Observatory and worked with the Botanical Expedition as a zoologist; of the execution of Miguel Pombo, a native of Popayán and nephew of Caldas's benefactor José Ignacio de Pombo; and perhaps of the execution of Joaquin Camacho, a contributor to the *Semanario*, and Caldas's collaborator on the *Diario Politico*.

In early October, in Bogotá, Camilo Torres was executed, decapitated and his head put in a cage for public viewing. And as Caldas was led through the mountain passes nearing the capital, Salvador Rizo, the director of the expedition's painters was put to death.

Thus when Caldas arrived at the village of Mesa de Juan Diaz, his last hope was to plead for mercy. He wrote to Pascual Enrile, Morillo's chief of staff. Presumably Enrile's status as a navigator and his responsibility for the works of the Expedition would have made him sympathetic to Caldas's case. In his letter Caldas repudiated his entire involvement in the revolution, noted that he had never actually fought against Spanish soldiers and implored, ". . . may Your Excellency take pity on me, on my unfortunate family and save me for the King."[12]

Caldas asked to be allowed to complete his unfinished projects, principally his works on plant geography and the geography of Nueva Granada. These, along with his hypsometric and cinchona memoirs, he claimed as ". . . original works, which would have honored the Botanical Expedition."[13] Caldas also had the presence of mind to claim to be the only person capable of organizing the manuscripts of José Celestino Mutis, a point that should have interested Enrile.

The plea had no effect. With cruel irony Caldas was imprisoned in the Colegio del Rosario, where he had been professor of mathematics. Pascual Enrile had Caldas questioned on 28 October about the letter and about other matters regarding the expedition. What mattered to the Spaniards was the recovery of what they regarded as Spanish property. The contributions of Caldas and other Granadians were ignored. Caldas's final effort to save his life and return to his work as a scientist had come to nothing.

On the morning of 29 October 1816 Caldas was led from his prison, and kneeling, was shot in the back by a firing squad.

---

12 Ibid., 355.
13 Ibid., 355.

EPILOGUE

The subjugation of Nueva Granada lasted only until 1819. Simón Bolivar returned and, building upon the group of patriots that had escaped to the province of Casanare, led a series of brilliant campaigns that brought liberty to Venezuela, Nueva Granada (Colombia, Ecuador and Panama), Peru and Bolivia. Although the Spanish decision to eliminate the revolutionary leadership had been carried out quickly and effectively, the desire for independence was not extinguished. On the contrary, the reign of terror showed the Granadians the true face of their enemy. In their darkest moment Creoles gained what they needed most – unity.

In the process of trying to reclaim its American colonies, Spain dealt a terrible blow to the nascent scientific community. The execution of a generation of intellectuals truncated the development of science and technology in the new nation. Furthermore, the Botanical Expedition was decisively disbanded. Having waited for years for José Celestino Mutis to publish his findings, the monarchy ordered its envoys to simply pack up and remit all of the expedition's materials. This task was given to Sinforoso Mutis who, perhaps owing to his lineage, was spared execution and sent to forced labor in Cartagena. For some thirty days, and under prison guard, Sinforoso packed one hundred and four (104) crates with the drawings, specimens, manuscripts and notes accumulated during thirty years of labor. The specimens were sent to Spain where they were subject to occasional inspection until in 1952 the governments of Spain and Colombia signed an agreement to publish the works of the Botanical Expedition.

Caldas's widow and his two daughters apparently lived out normal lives. There is little information available on them.

The loss of Caldas's notebooks and manuscripts might have occurred at any one of a number of junctures – the embargo placed by Nariño; the use of observatory equipment for Nariño's campaign in Popayán; the invasion of Bogotá by Bolivar's troops in 1815; the confiscation of Caldas's possessions by General Morillo in October 1816; or the difficulties faced by Manuela Barahona de Caldas following her husband's death.

Caldas's scientific career merits attention because he began as a scientist in search of community. He instinctively followed a path that brought him to the mainstream of the scientific enterprise, although ever distant from European science. Caldas began without books or equipment. He had no way of judging whether his studies dealt with phenomena known or new, and his makeshift instruments limited his ability to make more than rudimentary observations. His only correspondents were his understanding friends who could not offer the information, criticism or advice that scientists receive from their peers. Most importantly, as a solitary scientist Caldas found it difficult to chose a research program that he could carry out and that would produce original results.

It was Caldas's good fortune that Jose Celestino Mutis preceded him and that Humboldt and Bonpland befriended him. Otherwise, he would have remained an enlightened amateur. The Europeans were able to strengthen Caldas's intentions by reassuring him when he was doing well and teaching him much that he did not know. They also gave him a sense of the level of European science. Mutis directed Caldas toward the study of botany thus setting him on a course on which being in Nueva Granada was a positive factor. Furthermore, Mutis bestowed upon Caldas the Observatory, a prize that Caldas would never have gained as a scientist working in isolation. By entering in contact with a community of scientists, Caldas was able to define the direction of his work and gain the support and confidence to carry it out.

To conclude, what did Caldas's death mean for the scientific enterprise in Nueva Granada? Certainly, he had clearly stated his interest in the nation's geography and that of his ideas on plants. More important, Caldas brought personal and professional qualities to bear on the development of a scientific community.

Caldas was an active proponent of science. He had pressed prospective patrons for support, tried to motivate public interest and sought to attract students. He understood the need for communication between scientists. It is reasonable to suppose that had Caldas lived he would have revived his *Semanario* or some similar scientific journal. He would also have tried to open lines of communication with European scientists.

Caldas's interest was in science and not politics as many of his contemporaries in the Botanical Expedition were. Thus it is likely that Caldas would have been a constant supporter of science from a middle ground distant from political intrigues. Caldas knew that European science was the measure against which to be judged. He would have insisted on sending students to Europe, trying to compete with Europeans where that was possible. In short, Caldas was a scientist around whom a community could be started.

Clearly any judgment of what Caldas could have accomplished is conjecture. In addition, in attempting to judge Caldas's accomplishments one must remember that he was active as a scientist for only about ten years. Prior to 1810 he worked in isolation and following 1810 he lacked the tranquillity and support to maintain a program of investigation.

What then can be said of Caldas? Perhaps it is sufficient to note that in 1822, in a letter to Simón Bolivar, Baron Alexander von Humboldt remarked that he had begun the study of barometric measurements of altitude in Nueva Granada along with "the unfortunate Caldas."[1] That the baron was willing to give Caldas his due some twenty years after their meeting and six years after Caldas's death is tribute enough. It is a tragedy that such a man was not allowed to carry on his important work.

---

[1] Enrique Perez Arbelaez, ed. *Alejandro Humboldt en Colombia.* Instituto Colombiano de Cultura. Bogotá. 1982, p. 267.

APPENDIX A

DRAFT OF A NEW METHOD TO MEASURE THE ALTITUDE OF MOUNTAINS BY MEANS OF THE THERMOMETER AND BOILING WATER

By DON FRANCISCO JOSÉ DE CALDAS

1. During a brief trip[1] that we made to the Puracé Volcano, some five leagues to the east of Popayán, to study its mouth, altitude, snow line in this latitude, its many streams of mineral water and plants, I enjoyed no better incident than the bursting of a thermometer in the extreme end of the tube. Yes, this was the most inestimable result of that expedition, because it opened ideas in my soul that otherwise would never have been aroused.

2. Back in Popayán with only the thermometer that had just broken, with the pain of seeing interrupted a series of observations already underway, I tried to use what remained of this instrument. The freezing point, I thought, although it remains invariable will certainly lower as a result of the mercury that will be spilled when it boils; but we have snow all year and it is easy to determine the lower limit of my scale. In my first reflections I thought that the heat of boiling water would give me the same certainty for the upper limit. Without thinking more about the truth of these principles, I take rain water with precaution, I boil it, submerge my thermometer, let the excess mercury evacuate, close it and I conclude that I have a limit to my new scale. Then I order that snow be brought, crush it and wrap the bulb of the thermometer in it; I signal the point where it settles and I think that the only thing left to do is to divide the space between the two points into 80 parts if I want the Réamur scale, and into 180 if that of Fahrenheit. I experimented and I found some temperatures too low compared with those that the thermometer had before it broke. The heat of the atmosphere in Popayán, so well known to me from my previous observations, rises; and anyone not knowing this would have believed that this city had the same climate as Neiva or Mariquita. In general, I concluded that the limits of my scale were in error and that it was necessary to do further research. Could both points, of ice and boiling water be affected by some rare correction which I had omitted? Would snow be colder nearer the equator? Would the idea that ice is colder with latitude survive? I had taken care to submerge my thermometer in snow many times before it broke, and it always settled exactly at the freezing point. The opposite happened, my observations on this point confirmed more surely that it is

---

[1] The author of this trip was Don Antonio Arboleda, an intelligent youth and lover of useful knowledge. We were accompanied by Don Juan Jose Hurtado who is equally enthusiastic. We spent eight days assisted by remarkable [natural] grandeur and supplied with all that we needed. We wrote a Memoir on the Puracé Volcano; it contains the determination of the vegetation at a latitude of 2° 20′ N; thoughts on this point; analysis of two mineral springs; their description; two waterfalls; our geodesic observations; conjectures about the volcano's eruptions; and, finally, the descriptions of a considerable number of plants.

fixed than those of doctor Martine. This physicist[2] had only seen that ice was equally cold at 56°20′ and 52°30′ N. between which there is a difference of no more than 3°48′. But my work on this subject proves that my thermometer, which marks 0° in London at 51°30′ N, settles in the same point at 2°24′ N, when it is submerged in ice, and I have just learned that the same occurs in Quito at 13′ S. Ice, then, is equally cold below the equator and at 51°30′ N, that is, in a sea level country as in London and at an altitude of 800 toises in Popayán or at 1,600 toises above sea level as in Quito, countries so different in their climates as in their products that they represent extremes.

3. Though I had clear ideas and facts that determined the freezing point, I had thought very little about boiling water. From then on I knew that the error in the scale accrued over the upper limit, and I tried to determine exact notions about it, as I had of the lower limit. Suddenly, I saw that although the temperature of boiling water is constant, it supposes equal atmospheric pressure; that in raising or lowering this, one raises or lowers the water temperature; and, finally, that I was working at 800 toises above sea level, and with a pressure of only 22 inches 10.9 lines, the height of mercury in Popayán, instead of 28 in. that are required to obtain the upper limit of a correct scale. It was, then, necessary to increase the space between the two fundamental points, in the amount that corresponds to 5 in. 1.1 lines of increased pressure on the water. But, on what principles should I base my calculation? Very little or nothing has been written; or I should say, very little or nothing has come to my hands on this point. All physicists, all artisans close their thermometers when the barometer is at 28 in., and DeLuc adopts the height of 27 in. as more general in the cities of Europe. The only light, and that rather dim, that I had was in a passage in M. Sigaud de la Fond,[3] in which he says of doctor Martine: "This physicist has observed that the rise or descent of mercury being of one inch in the barometer, the temperature of boiling water varies something less than two degrees in the Fahrenheit scale." The expression, "something less," by not specifying an exact amount, puzzled me, and I realized the impossibility of verifying in my thermometer the upper limit of the scale without traveling to a lower place where my barometer would rise to 28 in. Though the need was crucial, I could not make such an expensive trip for this reason alone. I directed all my efforts to see if I could verify my scale without leaving Popayán.

4. Two degrees Fahrenheit equal 0.888° Réamur. Would the "something less" of Dr. Martine perhaps be the last two digits of the fraction just mentioned? I want to believe this to be the quantity assigned by this physicist; I want, for now, to calculate using only 0.8° Réamur for one barometric inch and so

$$12 \text{ lines} = 0.8°$$
$$5 \text{ in. } 1.1 \text{ lines} = 61.1 \text{ lines}$$
$$\frac{61.1 \times 0.8°}{12} = 4° \text{ R.}$$

I must, then, use this calculation; add 4.073° to the upper limit of the heat of boiling water in Popayán, and the unit that must serve to verify this quantity I find to be

$$80° - 4.073° = 75.927°$$

---

[2] Física Experimental by M. Sigaud, volume 3, page 195.
[3] Física Experimental, volume 3, page 89.

It follows that I must divide, at the altitude of Popayán, the space between ice and boiling water in 75.927° as that is the heat of this fluid at a pressure of 22 in. 10.9 lines.

5. Such were the results of my combinations, results which did not leave me satisfied. They were the product of two numbers that are not well known to us. The average height of the mercury in a barometer at sea level on the equator and nearby, and that amount by which the temperature of boiling water increases or decreases per inch of this instrument are uncertain quantities.

6. Despite the observations made by the astronomers Godin, Bouger, de la Condamine, Juan, Ulloa in Portobello, Panama, Manta and Guayaquil, we remain uncertain about the height of the barometer at sea level in the tropics. These savants stayed in our coastal areas for a limited time and the results of their observations vary. If we reflect upon what they have written, if we take the time to make comparisons and keep in mind what was known at that time, we will find that the variations are greater at lower elevations and much less in the climate of the mountains; that their measurements go from 27 in. 11 lines to 28 in. 1½ lines; that in 1735 and 36 one did not consider reducing the column of mercury dilated by 27, 28 and many times 29 degrees of heat in the Réamur scale; that it is doubtful they have taken the precaution of not deducing the altitude by means of the sum of all observations, divided by their number, a method which has exposed many observers to great errors and made useless so many important observations; and, finally, that the average altitude is that given by only one barometer, and never by many tubes of different density and caliber. What suspicions should not be raised by these considerations! I have dealt with this subject more thoroughly in a "Memoir regarding the average height of mercury at sea level in the tropics."

7. The other datum of my calculation is even more uncertain, and if I may speak with the ingenuousness of a lover of truth, my fraction−0.8° per 12 lines of the barometer−is a guess. From these principles which came to me with the conviction of truth, I concluded that the heat of water in Popayan was uncertain, independent of all suppositions.

8. I would have ended the struggle with my scale if I could have found a thermometer to substitute for the first one. The observations already made would then be rendered useless, and I have a powerful motive which animates me; I redouble my efforts, read the few physicists whose books I have, and begin to meditate seriously. One day, reviewing in my mind all of the ideas I had considered, I decide to retrace my steps to clarify them and take the path in reverse. "The heat of boiling water is proportional to the atmospheric pressure; the atmospheric pressure is proportional to the altitude above sea level; the atmospheric pressure follows the same law as the height of the barometer or, more properly speaking, the barometer shows us nothing other than the atmospheric pressure; therefore the heat of water indicates the atmospheric pressure in the same way as the barometer; therefore it can give us the altitudes of places without the necessity of a barometer and with equal certainty." Could this be a true discovery? Could I, in the unlearned climate of Popayán, have uncovered a method already found and perfected by some European sage? Or, on the contrary, could I be the first to have had these ideas? Being so clear, could they have hidden from Réamur, Delisle, Fahrenheit, DeLuc and Sucio [Saussure]? The most recent book I have is Sigaud; consulting it again, I find nothing similar to my theory. It does indicate a method of measuring altitudes by thermometer, but how different, how imperfect! Would he have ignored the heat of water if he had known of it at the time he wrote? At least I can conclude that up to this point he had not thought about it. The simplicity of the principles, the clarity of the ideas caused me, despite these considerations, great misgivings. Is it possible—I ask myself again—that the small details have remained hidden from great men? It is true that history presents us with examples that cannot be read without embarrassment. Who could believe that the ancients who possessed the art of glassmaking did not use it to defend themselves from air and cold without shutting out the light? That the Peruvians who erected buildings that we admire did not know how to form windows? It could be that these sages, always occupied by greater problems, have missed these ideas. What doubts! How sad is the fate of an American! After much work, if he happens to find something new, the most he can say is—it is not in my books. Can any people of the Earth grow wise without a speedier communication with civilized Europe? What darkness surrounds us! Ah, but now we doubt, now we begin to work, now we hope. That is having come halfway. Who is the beneficent genius who has guided us thus far? Mutis arrives at our coasts, light shines over our hemisphere, the cry is raised and this lethargic world is awakened. Illustrious sage, I see you in this moment surrounded by a glory that even your most implacable enemies cannot take away; you brought us the first notions of science; if we are still not sages it is no fault of yours; all must be imputed to our laziness and to that lamentable fidelity to ancient preoccupations. If, in correspondence with your fatherly guidance, we follow the glorious path you have opened; if the sciences make progress among us; if someone wants to reproduce Montucla, Baille and Andres in the New World; if the literary history of America is written, you will be at the forefront, you will be the father of our enlightenment. I have changed course without notice, I have come to the object of my love and my delirium. My countrymen, the youths who aspire to wisdom, would that—forgetting the subject of this draft of a Memoir—it become a panegyric of the author of their enlightenment. Such a purpose! Such a hero! I tremble, I do not dare touch him. The ashes of Fontenelle and Tomas; the ingenious successors of these sages would reclaim their rights; I will not dispute them; into your hands I put a subject that is not worthy of mine; I will content myself with not having yielded to them in my zeal, and with speaking of boiling water and the thermometer.

9. Whether known or new I must perfect them—I said to myself—I must rely on experience. If the first be the case we will have an example of the same facts coming at the same time to many; we will compare the work of the European with that of the son of Popayán; we will see the paths they have followed, their results and perhaps the work one will correct the others, perfecting this theory. Even if they had given proof beyond doubt, I will not have wasted my work. In that case, my observations will be confirmation; they will prove its universality; that below the line, at low latitudes, at all altitudes, the results are the same as in the temperate zone and are not affected by distance or climate. If the latter be the case, is it not—I say—reprehensible laziness to abandon a subject that can yield important results?

10. These thoughts inspire in me a courage to overcome the obstacles which surround me, they make me resolve to work as much as I can. But, where should I begin? What principles should guide me in my investigations? Solitary, isolated, without enlightenment, without books, without instruments, I must build by my

own hand, I must be the creator of all that is necessary to continue in the projected work. The first must be the observation of the heat of water in Popayán with an exact thermometer. What a difficulty! I have yet to begin; my work is always detained. Nothing stops me; I question with the utmost care if there is a thermometer in Popayán and who has it. I discover two, one of spirit which is of no use to me; the other, of mercury, is the one I need. I find it without difficulty. It is one made by Dollond and manufactured in London. I examine the freezing point and find it to be exact. I cannot equally examine the upper limit and suppose it to be correct; I divide the fundamental space in 80°; adapt a vernier that subdivides each degree in ten parts; take rain water, boil it, submerge the thermometer, fan the fire, and the mercury stops—fixed at 75.7°. I jump with pleasure; how close to my first conjectures![4] My ideas begin to be confirmed by experiment. I put aside my scruples for now, adopt 28 in. for the barometer at sea level and 80° for the thermometer for the heat of water at this pressure; I know the values in Popayán to be 75.7° and 22 in. 10.9 lines; I then calculate what the variation per inch of barometer should be[5]

$$28 \text{ in.} - 22 \text{ in. } 11 \text{ lines} = 5 \text{ in. } 1 \text{ line} = 61 \text{ lines}$$
$$80° - 75.7° = 4.3°$$
$$61 \text{ lines: } 4.3° :: 12 \text{ lines}$$
$$\frac{12 \times 4.3°}{61} = 0.8°$$

±0.8° in the thermometer of Réamur per ±12 lines in the barometer. How well had I supposed the "something less" of Dr. Martine.[6]

11. With this result I begin the inverse calculation. I start from it [the factor 0.8° R per inch] and from the heat of water in Popayán calculate the corresponding height of the barometer

$$0.8° : 12 \text{ lines} :: 4.3°$$
$$\frac{4.3 \times 12}{0.8} = 64 \text{ lines} = 5 \text{ in. } 4 \text{ lines}$$
$$28 \text{ in.} - 5 \text{ in. } 4 \text{ lines} = 22 \text{ in. } 8 \text{ lines}$$

the height of mercury in the barometer, corresponding to Popayan. This does not differ from what is indicated by this instrument by more than 2.9 lines. This result is more precise than I had expected, but does not satisfy me. How many errors in principle come to mind! The impurity of water, the form of the recipient, the height of the barometer in our seas, the exponent, the scale and above all the lack of practice I have in experiences of this type; these afflict me; I am ashamed of my laxity; I scold myself; I have new thoughts; to remove obstacles I distinguish the sources of error which are insurmountable from those that are not; only the value of the barometer at sea level is among the former; the latter demand only patience and work for their elimination.

12. Presently a friend[7] invites me to a beautiful country home he owns in the slopes of the famous cordillera of the Andes, and located at many toises above the level of Popayán. I do not miss the opportunity. Telling my friend of my ideas,

---

4 See section 4 of this draft.
5 Rounding off, because 0.1° can be dropped in our case and would otherwise complicate the calculation.
6 See section 4.
7 Doctor Don Manuel Maria Arboleda, vicar general of the bishop of Popayán.

I find him favorably disposed and equally animated; we depart with our instruments. What enterprise, what devotion of this companion to my efforts! He shuns not even the most arduous and humble tasks. Despite the barbarous education he received in his youth, he has been able to shake off preoccupations, he knows the path of truth, he works with purpose. Books, instruments, enlightenment here is the object of his ambition. How much do I owe this generous friend! Half of the glory, if these small efforts are worth it, belong to him. I am sure that had he not helped me in person and with his money, my ideas would be buried in oblivion. I would fail the laws of decency were I not to give acknowledgment of my gratitude and love.

13. We make many experiments in Poblazón;[8] scaling a nearby peak named Buenavista; we observe the heat of water; the results are approximate and have the same degree of precision as in Popayán. New tests highlight the uncertainty of the average barometric height at sea level. Such a necessary element for my investigations! How can I assure myself, how can I know exactly the height of this column in our coasts. Verify it by going there, or direct the calculation so that I do not need to. I take this route and the method of execution is as follows.

14. I make Popayán the center of my operations; I make a scrupulous and certain determination of the average height of the mercury in this city; I determine, through repeated experiments, the heat of distilled water at this level; I refer my observations to this [value] and banish from my calculations the principle of 28 in. at sea level. When, by means of new and exact observations, we determine this fundamental principle, we have only to apply it, without changing at all the results of my observations.

15. The calculations relative to the level of Popayán, using the exponent 0.8 show the need to increase it [the factor 0.8] and I decide on a trip to the cordillera. I correct my instruments once again; I distill water, which I subject to the tests of silver solution (silver nitrate) and mercury solution (mercury nitrate), and equipped with what is necessary I depart on 22 July 1801.

16. Before presenting the results of my efforts on this famous mountain chain, one should know that the height of the barometer in Popayán, using the utmost care in my latest observations is 22 in. 11.2 lines, that is to say 0.3 lines greater than the value we had assigned earlier, and that the heat of water at this pressure is 75.65° on the Réamur scale.

17. In the place known as Las Juntas I make my first observation. The barometer here rose to 21 in. 9 lines, or 14 lines lower than in Popayán. I boil the water; the liquid of the thermometer stops at 74.5°. I calculate the exponent for this observation.

Height of barometer

In Popayán	22 in. 11.2 lines	Heat of water	75.65°
In Las Juntas	21 in. 9.0 lines		74.50°
Differences	1 in. 2.2 lines		1.15°

1 in. 2.2 lines: 1.15 : $\dfrac{12 \times 1.15}{14.2}$ = 0.971° Réamur per 12 lines on the barometer.

---

[8] This is the name of my friend's country home, three leagues east of Popayán.

18. I climb a little more, making my second observation in Paispamba, a small hacienda some five leagues south of Popayán. The barometer rises to 20 in. 9.1 lines and the heat of water is 73.5°.

Height of barometer

In Popayán	22 in. 11.2 lines	Heat of water	75.65°
In Paispamba	20 in. 9.1 lines		73.50°
Differences	2 in. 2.1 lines		2.15°

2 in. 2.1 lines = 26.1 lines: 2.15 : 12 lines: $\dfrac{12 \times 2.15}{26.1}$

$\qquad\qquad$ = 0.988° Réamur per 12 lines of the barometer.

19. I was extremely happy seeing the result of the second observation. What conformity in the exponent! It differs from the first only by 0.017, a quantity which cannot be indicated by the most delicate of instruments.

20. Enlivened by such good results, I take one more step: I climb a peak east of Paispamba, known as Sombreros; the barometer marks 19 in. 6.05 lines; the water boils at 72.4°

Height of barometer

In Popayán	22 in. 11.2 lines	Heat of water	75.65°
In Sombreros	19 in. 6.05 lines		72.40°
Differences	3 in. 5.15 lines		3.25°

3 in. 5.15 lines = 41.15 lines: 3.25 : 12 lines: $\dfrac{12 \times 3.25}{41.15}$

$\qquad\qquad$ = 0.948° Réamur per 12 lines of the barometer.

21. Here I have a result that agrees with the others, I have three observations which show that more than nine-tenths of a degree in the Réamur thermometer ± in the heat of water, correspond to 12 lines of the barometer.

22. I decide to climb more and arrive at the top of another peak called Tambores. The barometer here marks 18 in. 11.6 lines; the water marks 71.75°.

Height of barometer

In Popayán	22 in. 11.2 lines	Heat of water	75.65°
In Tambores	18 in. 11.6 lines		71.75°
Differences	3 in. 11.6 lines		3.90°

3 in. 11.6 lines = 47.6 lines: 3.9 :: 12 lines: $\dfrac{12 \times 3.90}{47.6}$

$\qquad\qquad$ = 0.983° Réamur per 12 lines of the barometer.

23. I am satisfied seeing this last number; my doubts fade; I confirm the uncertainty of the height of the barometer at sea level and know that more than nine-tenths is the true exponent; that the pressure indicated by the barometer does not differ from that of the heat of water; and, finally, that my ideas are confirmed by experiment.

24. I start over, combining the most satisfactory results. I select them prudently and with caution, since the object is to determine an exponent which will be the basis of later calculations. I take the observations of Las Juntas and Sombreros, and calculate the exponent once again.

Height of barometer

In Las Juntas	21 in. 9.00 lines	Heat of water	74.60°
In Sombreros	19 in. 6.05 lines		72.40°
Differences	2 in. 2.95 lines		2.20°

2 in. 2.95 lines = 26.95 lines: 2.20 :: 12 lines: $\dfrac{12 \times 2.20}{26.95}$

$\qquad$ = 0.979° Réamur per 12 lines of the barometer.

25. I do the same with the observations of Paispamba and Tambores.

Height of barometer

In Paispamba	20 in. 9.1 lines	Heat of water	73.50°
In Tambores	18 in. 11.6 lines		71.75°
Differences	1 in. 9.5 lines		1.75°

1 in. 9.5 lines = 21.5 lines: 1.75 :: 12 lines: $\dfrac{12 \times 1.75}{21.5}$

$\qquad$ = 0.976° Réamur per 12 lines of the barometer

26. There is no doubt now that the true coefficient is more than nine-tenths. Let us examine, then, this important element. I add the six results, divide by their number and the quotient 0.974 is the number we look for, that which expresses the quantity ± in the Réamur thermometer per 12 lines of the barometer.

27. Now we can solve the problem. Given the heat of boiling water at a site, find the corresponding height of the barometer and the altitude above sea level.

28. The difference of the heat of water at a site relative to Popayán for now, or to sea level when that is known, varies as the exponent of 0.974 :: 12 lines. If a site is above the level of Popayán, some number of inches, lines, etc. of the barometer will be subtracted; they will be added if the place is below Popayán; with respect to sea level the height of mercury will always be less. Let us test the application of these principles.

29. The heat of water in Tambores is 71.75°; we seek the corresponding barometric height.

Heat of water	In Popayán	75.65°
	In Tambores	71.75°
	Difference	3.90°

0.974: 12 lines: 3.90 :: $\dfrac{3.90 \times 12}{0.974}$ = 48.05 lines = 4 in. 0.05 lines

Since Tambores is above the level of Popayán, I subtract this result from the height of the barometer in that city.

Height of barometer in Popayán	22 in. 11.20 lines
Result	4 in. 00.05 lines
Remainder	18 in. 11.15 lines

$\qquad$ Let us compare the result of this calculation with the observations I made on this peak.

Height of barometer in Tambores	18 in. 11.60 lines
Height of barometer calculated by the heat of water	18 in. 11.15 lines
Difference	00 in. 00.45 lines

30. Greater accuracy cannot be obtained. If we want a general equation for this calculation, let us use:

a = height of the barometer in Popayán or at sea level.
b = heat of water in these places.
c = the exponent.
e = 12 lines.
d = heat of water in a given location.
z = height of the barometer in that place.

Reasoning as we did before, we have

$$a + \frac{(b - d)e}{-c} = z \quad \text{with reference to Popayán}$$

$$a - \frac{(b - d)e}{c} = z \quad \text{with reference to sea level}$$

31. Following these principles I have calculated the heights of the barometer corresponding to those places where I have observed the heat of water, which I have mentioned, and others which I observed when I returned to Popayán. The following table shows immediately the heat of water in the Réamur and Fahrenheit scales, the barometric heights observed and those calculated by the heat of water, and the differences between them.

Locations	Heat of Water T(R)	T(F)	Barometric Heights Observed	Calculated	Difference
Popayán	75.65	202.21	22 in. 11.2		
Juntas	74.50	199.62	21 in. 9.0	21 in. 9.04	+0.04
Paispamba	73.50	197.37	20 in. 9.1	20 in. 8.72	−0.38
Sombreros	72.40	194.90	19 in. 6.05	19 in. 7.15	+1.10
Tambores	71.75	193.43	18 in. 11.6	18 in. 11.15	−0.45
Estrellas	73.30	196.87	20 in. 7.0	20 in. 6.25	−0.75
Poblazon	74.30	199.17	21 in. 6.9	21 in. 6.59	−0.31
Buenavista	73.80	197.05	21 in. 1.15	21 in. 0.5	−0.65

32. These seven observations of the heat of water, seven barometric heights calculated from them and compared with observations, which do not differ in amounts greater than that which our instruments can indicate, and which in six observations do not show one line of error and in the other does not pass 1.1 line, show a sure method of measuring the elevations of places without the aid of the barometer.

33. This was the state of my work when private matters forced me to travel to Quito. I was happy to be able to reproduce my observations in so many different levels in those areas through which I would have to pass. Despite my best efforts, I could only make three: one in the burning Valley of Patia, another in Pasto and the last in Quito. I would not have verified even these if not for the help of an illustrious and zealous friend,[9] who was my only traveling companion. I cannot omit mentioning him as a demonstration of my recognition. The following table at once presents the results.

---

[9] Don Toribio Miguel Rodriguez, lawyer in Quito.

| Locations | Heat of Water | | Barometric Heights | | Difference |
	T(R)	T(F)	Observed	Calculated	
Herradura	78.50	208.62	25 in. 11.85	25 in. 10.31	− 1.54
Pasto	73.60	197.60	20 in. 9.85	20 in. 9.95	+ 0.10
Quito	73.05	196.30	20 in. 2.00	20 in. 3.18	+ 1.18

34. Baron Humboldt's arrival was imminent, and I wait impatiently for this young sage to clear up my doubts. In conversation with him I confirm that the average height of mercury at sea level near the equator is uncertain and that we can absolutely ignore the heat of water there. I explain my method to him and ask if it is new. This sage first thinks that Sucio[10] has worked with this idea; he checks his manuscripts and answers: "Sucio has not thought of boiling water as you have; his work is limited to the atmospheric temperature; he assigns 640 feet of altitude per degree of the thermometer, and I have observed in Pico de Teide that this coefficient works well when the day is calm and one does not work in elevated places." Instantly I know I have made if, it can be so called, a small discovery. Such a difference between the Sucio's method and mine! How imperfect the first! How untenable! Sucio has only perfected the ideas of Heberden,[11] ideas exposed to the most flagrant errors, nearly impracticable and which demand the judgment and prudence of an accomplished physicist to apply them with success. How is it possible that the temperature of the atmosphere, with infinite variations in one same level influenced by location, reflection, wind, clouds, the time of day, can be used with certainty for the determination of the altitude? Even if you suppose two people observing at the same time, how many particular factors in each station may alter the liquid of the thermometer? How rare, how difficult it is to find a calm day! And this one condition, how it limits the method of Heberden and Sucio! Observing boiling water, however, gives all the convenience, all the precision that could be asked. Let the day be calm, cloudy, cold, hot, windy; let the observer be covered or exposed; the boiling water will always indicate in the thermometer a heat proportional to the pressure.

35. Furthermore, the coefficient of 640 feet per degree, is, for the barometer, a coefficient relative to altitude, and must necessarily vary in the lower, middle and higher zones, without which the method is exposed to gross errors and in contradiction to theory. This constant coefficient has the same effect as if we gave one to the barometer, as does Paulian, assigning 12 toises of altitude per line of reduction in this instrument. One must be an uninitiated in physics to admit such an erroneous principle. The work done in Quito at the beginning of the last century shows that, for the elevation of Caraburu, it is necessary to climb 17 toises so that the barometer lowers by one line. I consider that any constant coefficient relative to altitude to be absurd.

36. These defects cannot be attributed to my coefficient. It is relative to the pressure, and rises in height where that is reduced. It is relative to the barometer, and all the investigation regarding that law and the progress made with that instrument are accommodated by the heat of water, since neither has any basis different from that of atmospheric pressure. Baron von Humboldt, to whom I have shown my ideas, thought that my coefficient had the same defects as that

---

10 [Author's note: Here Caldas means Horace Benedict Saussure.]
11 [Author's note: William Heberden. See Chapter Two.]

of Sucio; but upon further thought, agreed with me about the precision of my coefficient, which distinguishes it from others.

37. This sage objected that the heat of [boiling] water varied, at the same pressure, by as much as one degree. I would have happily subscribed to such a respected authority; if authority matched experience. Experience has taught me that the heat of water at equal pressure is invariable, if one takes precautions. The opinion of all physicists supports my view. If this were not so, could there exist comparable thermometers? Is not the invariability of the heat of boiling water at 28 in. of pressure the basis of the upper limit of the scale of all thermometers? It is true that at first boiling the water has not acquired all the heat of which it is capable, but, fanning the flames, increasing the boiling to its maximum, it always acquires the same heat.

38. One might think that this method requires large thermometers to obtain the pressure; but I have already noted what experience has taught me about this point. The thermometer I have used for all my observations has a length of ll inches 1 line of the foot of the king, and each degree of the scale of Réamur, 1 inch 15 lines, a space too great to admit considerable subdivision. By means of a vernier I have divided each degree in ten parts and can read up to half of one-tenth with great clarity. The results of my experiences have such a degree of precision, that the major differences do not pass 1½ lines of the barometer; and I hope to correct this difference with later observations made with more and better instruments.

39. I have noted the errors that can be made with this scale, and I have found that if the observer is so careless as to err by 0.1° in the thermometer, only 1.25 lines of variation will be produced in the barometer. If one notes that it is very difficult to err by this quantity, working with caution and care, it is clear that the method of the heat of water is as exact as that of the barometer and perhaps more; finally, that it should be put into practice.

40. All who have some experience using the barometer agree that it is an instrument difficult to transport—voluminous, much more exposed than the thermometer and that to prepare it demands great care and attention, which the ordinary person is not capable of giving it. How much intelligence does it require just for the purification of mercury? If we add to that the preparation of the tube, the manner of filling it, the elimination of air, the scale, the calibration, we can see that this instrument can only be trusted to the physicists; it can never become of common use and observations with it will not increase because this knowledge will never become common. The thermometer costs little, is easy to transport, there is no purification, no filling, no air to eliminate, no calibration; that is, it does not need, as does the barometer, an auxiliary instrument to obtain precise results.

41. The method of observation by the heat of water can be simplified such that the most ignorant, the least versed in the study of physics can observe and calculate elevations by himself. Adding to the thermometer a scale which indicates the inches of the barometer, the calculations shown above are needless and can be suppressed.

42. I have now discussed the scale and the principles to be used. The fraction 0.974° on the Réamur scale equals 12 lines or 1 inch of the barometer. If one multiplies by 12, 13, 14, etc. until one finds a product without fractions, or with, but easy to establish with a compass and one takes for the thermometer scale as many degrees as there are units of the multiplier, one finds the extremes of the thermometer. Let us make this clearer. The product of 0.974° with 19 is 18.506°; let us drop the .006 as a quantity infinitely small and not notable in practice; we will have that 18.5° of the Réamur scale correspond to 19 in. of the barometer. I take 18.5° on the thermometer scale; I pass them on the left-hand side from the superior limit down; I divide this space in 19 parts, and the barometric inches are now expressed on the thermometer; I apply a vernier which subdivides these in 20 parts and I have a scale which gives me divisions of half a line of the barometer. If one does not subscribe to these principles, one must not have paid close attention. There is no barometer next to a barometer, no tube alongside another tube. Their differences in the same place, with the same mercury, the same scale may come to 4½ lines; considerable difference, caused by the caliber and attractions to which neither the thermometer nor the method of the heat of water are subject. I am aware of the variations to which thermometers manufactured by the same method are exposed; but compared with those of the barometer it seems to me that the results of the thermometer are more uniform than those of the barometer. If the disadvantages in which my limited fortunes have immured me had not intervened; if the obstacles would have been less, I would speak now more positively, I could evaluate the errors and compare them; but I cannot; I have lacked instruments, means, occasion.

43. The adjoining figure [Fig. 2, page 13] represents my thermometer in its true size; in it is seen more clearly the common scale for heat and that which indicates the height of the barometer. Have we united in one small instrument the celebrated discoveries of Drobbel and Torricelli? The sages and experience, will decide.

44. This is not a memoir, it is a draft from which to make one. How much effort, how many observations are needed to give it the final touch! How many details, omitted owing to the lack of instruments, must be observed! I have not been able to correct the barometric measurements made in Popayán, Poblazón, Juntas, Tambores, etc. for the effects of heat and cold, because I lacked a thermometer to indicate the temperature of the atmosphere when my only thermometer marked the heat of water. Who knows if the small differences I have found are caused by a lack of rectification!

45. When I think that for little cost and in a short time one can give this subject the highest possible degree of accuracy; when I find myself in the neighborhood of the most beautiful place one can find on earth, which appears formed by nature with this intention, I become anxious and burn with eagerness to verify my ideas as soon as possible. Chimborazo, this colossal mass, located at two and one-half degrees latitude south, whose flanks descend directly to the Pacific coast and through which lies the road which links Quito with the port of Guayaquil, presents all of the area and all of the comfort imaginable to observe the heat of water from the snow line to sea level. If it is true that the thermometer marks 16 inches in the former, one can make 12 observations, inch by inch, until number 28 in Guayaquil. Here, measuring the average height and the heat of water at the very coast, the basis of a theory would be made, one could perfect the simplest, least expensive and perhaps the surest method of measuring the elevation of mountains and all other places.

46. The benefits seem clear. There is hardly a city, hardly a town where one does not find someone with a thermometer; this is without a doubt the instrument most generally used. One can say that for every hundred thermometers there is but one barometer; the method is easy, the observation simple and within reach of the common man. What wonderful expectations I have, that within a short number of years we can know the elevations of all nations! This set of procedures, what great knowledge it will give us about the form of the continents, about the currents of water, about the mysterious revolutions of this crust of the globe that we inhabit! This material, in the hands of the wise successors of Wooduar and Buffon, will produce a theory of the Earth that is on a better basis, less imaginative, more catholic.

47. When, through a series of observations, I have compared the heat of distilled water with that of rainwater; when I have put the final touch to my Memoir regarding the precautions that must be taken with this type of observation, we will have arrived at the point where we need only a simple thermometer and rain to measure all the mountains, all the valleys and all places. If we compare this with spring water, we will have doubled the ease of observation. If it is found that pure water is not needed for relative altitudes, this method will not be the less for it. So many enthusiastic youths, who, lacking barometers, are eager for work—with how many observations will they enrich us! Now I see you all in motion, climbing treacherous mountains with your thermometers, descending gradually to the floor of burning valleys, constructing elevations for the four corners of the world and with them overturning the systems of some philosophers, building new ones on their ruins, lifting the veil slightly and taking geology a step forward. But this is too much, we barely know the present, what can we say of the future? Let us not usurp the rights of posterity. We aspire to its recognition or, at least, that we not be accused of indolence.

Appendix

I WOULD NOT WANT TO LOSE the auspicious occasion to compare my miserable instruments with those of Baron von Humboldt, and to do the same with the observations made in the same places. We had both observed the heat of water only in Popayán. This illustrious traveler found that with rainwater the thermometer marked 203.3° Fahrenheit in this city, whereas distilled water gave me 202.21°, that is, nearly a degree less. I was surprised to see such an enormous difference, since rainwater cannot produce one degree more in the thermometer. Could the error be—I asked myself—in our instruments? If it is, surely it must be caused by my thermometer. Hoping to remove the doubt, I ask the Baron to lend me the thermometer he used in Popayán for his observation. He lets me take it home and I place it beside mine; allow them to reach room temperature, and find that the Baron's is exactly one degree higher than mine. But which of the two gives the true temperature? The best way to achieve certainty is by using ice. I submerge both thermometers in it and note with satisfaction that the beautiful Nairne thermometer stops one degree above freezing or 33° Fahrenheit, while mine drops exactly to 0° Réamur and 32° Fahrenheit. It follows that it is necessary to subtract 1° from the results of the observations made with his instrument. Thus 203.3° − 1.0° = 202.3°, and taking off 0.1° for the use of rainwater, our observations are in perfect agreement; that of the Baron would be 202.20° and mine 202.21°. Here are two thermometers of different scales that give the same heat at the same level, even though our barometers give different readings. The Baron found that his barometer marked 23 in. 3.4 lines in Popayán; mine marked 22 in.

11.7 lines; and that of Bouger marked 22 in. 10.7 lines, nearly 5 lines lower than the first. Which thermometer made with precision would have such a difference? Ah, it seems that experience begins to confirm that the heat of water in different thermometers is more constant, less variable than the column of mercury in different barometers.

Another of Humboldt's observations that significantly confirms my ideas is that of the heat of water in Santa Fe. I have noted that his thermometer rose in the capital to 198.6° Fahrenheit; if we subtract one degree for instrument error, we have 197.6° − 0.1°, since it was spring water; we will have 195.5° as the heat of water in Santa Fe, which equals 73.55° Réamur. Let us calculate with this heat the altitude which my barometer should have given in this city.

Heat of water in Popayán   75.65°
In Santa Fe   73.55°
Difference   2.10°

$$0.974 : 12 :: 2.1 : \frac{2.1 \times 12}{0.974} = 25.8 \text{ lines}$$

$$= 2 \text{ in. } 1.8 \text{ lines less than in Popayán.}$$

Height of the barometer in Popayán   22 in. 11.2 lines
                                                                  −   2 in.   1.8 lines
Height of my barometer in Santa Fe   20 in. 9.4 lines

In 1796 I observed and published (*Correo Curioso*) that my barometer in this city marked 20 in. 8.0 lines at its highest level. The calculation and observation differ by only 1.4 lines, and there are no barometers which will show less variation between themselves.

We can do the same with Guadelupe. The Baron found that the heat of water on this peak is 194.6°

                        minus   −   1.1°
                        leaves   =   193.5°
            which equals =   71.77° Réamur.

Heat of water in Popayán   75.65°
            In Guadelupe   71.77°
            Difference   3.88°

$$0.974 : 12 :: 3.88° : \frac{3.88 \times 12}{0.974} = 47.8 \text{ lines}$$

$$= 3 \text{ in. } 11.8 \text{ lines less than in Popayán.}$$

Height of the barometer in Popayán   22 in. 11.2 lines
                                                                  − 3 in. 11.8 lines
Height of my barometer in Guadelupe   18 in. 11.4 lines

In 1796 I found exactly 19 inches (*Correo Curioso*), which differs from the calculation only by 0.6 lines. One cannot expect greater accuracy.

Quito. April 1802.

APPENDIX B

[Note: This is Caldas's initial work on the subject of plant geography. Although he often mentioned that he was preparing a more extensive study, none was ever published, nor did his manuscripts survive the turbulence of the revolutionary period. I have not found the map to which Caldas refers. The article is accompanied by a table of the altitudes of different towns which will not be included here.]

Memoir on the Distribution of Plants That Are Cultivated Near the Equator

In all of the small trips I have been able to make within the Viceroyalty of Santafé, my first concern has been to observe the altitude, the quantity and the limits which mark the cultivation of useful plants and on which we depend for our substinence. Since 1796, when I began to reflect upon these matters, until today (April 1803), I have compiled a considerable number of observations and facts; I have compared them, put this material in order, and believe that I now can determine some general results. This is not a finished work that I am presenting: I understand that we are very far from perfection, that we lack facts and that we do not have the necessary number of observations to give the final touch to the distribution of plants that are cultivated near the equator. This science, which scarcely exists in name, should be the first object of our travellers and of the observers that live in the different towns of the Viceroyalty; the utility and the advantages for our agriculture of this type of work are well-known by all and so I need not enter into a detailed discussion.

The accompanying plan[1] represents (sideview) all of the terrain covered by my observations: it starts from 4° 36' northern latitude to 0° southern latitude; that is to say, from Santafé [Bogotá] to Quito. The horizontal distances of the different points have been reduced considerably, because it would require a great length to represent two hundred leagues on the same scale as the altitudes above sea level, the greatest of which does not exceed 2,400 toises. More space has been given to those areas in cultivation, and the space accorded those areas that do not produce, or neglect, the plants considered in this Memoir has been reduced. Thus, the valleys of Neiva and Patia are greatly reduced, while those of Santafé [Bogotá], Popayán, Pasto, Pastos, Ibarra and Quito occupy a considerable area. From this alteration of horizontal differences comes inevitably the form of the mountains; and one cannot expect other than an imperfect image or shadow of that which really exists. As I have taken liberty in the reduction and accommodation of distances, I have been scrupulous in maintaining heights, to present the towns, mountains and valleys at their true altitude. I assume, with Bouger and

---

[1] Author's note: I have not found this plan, but it was probably similar to the graph made by Humboldt (Fig. 6, page 54) which Caldas held while writing this manuscript; and Caldas's own cinchona graph (Fig. 7, page 56).

with Humboldt, that along our coasts mercury [in the barometer] is sustained between 28 inches and 28 inches and 2 lines; and dropping the small fractions found in the works of these sage travellers, I take 28 inches exactly at the altitude of our seas. In divisions of inch by barometric inch are drawn horizontal lines parallel to the first, and in this way I represent the different layers of air or zones that make up the atmosphere. From line to line is marked a number that expresses the toises that one must climb so that the barometer's mercury drops one inch, or equally, the number of toises of altitude corresponding to each layer of atmospheric fluid.

I could well have calculated directly the elevation of each point above sea level, using the recent determination of the height of mercury at the Pacific coast by Humboldt and the formula perfected by Trailles, which this sage uses and which I owe to his generosity; but, I have preferred another route which combines simplicity with an exactness sufficient for these matters. The altitude of Quito is well known to us from the labors of the academics of the trip to the equator [see Chapter I], and has not been altered by the later investigations of Humboldt; I have drawn, then, a pointed line at 1,460 toises above sea level, and have calculated relative to it the altitude or depression of the different points which make up this distribution. For this I have used the very simple formula of Bouger[2] which gives a precision greater than that which is needed.

In all of the extension covered by this distribution wheat is cultivated only beginning at 22 inches of barometer or from 1,112 toises above sea level. From this level on down this precious plant is not seen again in our fields. I have drawn a line made up of small inclined dashes which I have called the lower limit of wheat to make it more apparent.

It is believed that this limit was determined by our first farmers, from whom we received it and maintained it without consideration; from this concept we are counseled to lower the planting of wheat to our coasts for which we are promised great advantages. But does this notion have a basis? I have here some questions which deserve to be examined.

If only we appeal to reason, there is no doubt that we will see this lower limit for the cultivation of wheat as a generalized preoccupation throughout the Viceroyalty. We know that in Europe, from where this plant was brought by the Spaniards, it is grown at very low altitudes and nearly along the coast; that vegetation grows and accelerates in proportion to the heat and humidity; and that wheat, far from prospering in deep cold, deteriorates to the point of being absolutely useless to men. The conquistadores planted it, and took abundant harvests in the first places of which they took possession in our continent, and did not wait for the conquest of the highlands of Leiva, Bogotá, Pasto and Quito to cultivate

---

[2] Let a = the height of mercury in Quito
　　　b = the height of mercury in any other point with (+) or with (−) minus
　　　　　depending if it is greater or lesser than that of Quito
　　　d = the difference
　　　x = the number of toises, plus or minus, above or below Quito

$$\text{Log } a - \text{Log } b = d \quad \text{or} \quad \text{Log } b - \text{Log } a = d$$

$$d - d/30 = x \text{ toises}$$

Example:　Height of mercury in Chinguiltina = 247.3 lines　　　　Log = 2.3932
　　　　　Height of mercury in Quito = 243 lines　　　　　　　　Log = 2.3856
　　　　　　　　　　　　　　　　　　　　　　　　　　　　　　　　────────
Difference, toises 76/30 = 2 toises 3.2 feet　　　　　　　　　　　76
76 t. − 2 t. 3.2 ft. = 73 toises 2.8 feet
Chinguiltina below the level of Quito.

it. It is certain that Cartagena, Santa Marta, Caracas as well as Quito and Bogotá have produced this precious grain which we find reduced to narrow limits today; perhaps, as with maize, two large harvests a year were collected in our tropical climates, instead of the lone harvest we now find in our temperate zone. History and the concert of reason would seem to condemn the present practice and to authorize the cultivation of wheat in the low, hot areas. But, if instead of reading and meditating, we approach those simple and virtuous men who are more comfortable with plow and hoe than with books, those eternal observers of nature, who seeing her constantly at hand know her better than do the philosophers who only look at intervals and from afar, we will find that the practice they observe is the best that can be established in our countries, and that our reasoning is erroneous and our condemnations unjust, and we will receive an important lesson that will shame our discussions when thay are not supported by good observations in matters of cultivation and should attend facts and not philosophy.

The mold or blight that we know by the name of *polvillo*, that terrible disease of the most beautiful of the grains is what has obliged our laborers to retire from the coasts and raise themselves to 1,112 toises above sea level. The judicious men, Targioni or Fontana, have shown the knowledgeable world that the *polvillo* is nothing other than a parasitic plant, similar to moss, that multiplies prodigiously as do all microscopic plants, attacking the cane and the stem of the wheat, and robs it of the fluids that were to feed the grain, weakening and killing it. At the same time that the heat and the humidity favor the growth and well-being of the wheat, they also favor the growth of this invisible and destructive plant; and extensive experience, verified in all places, teaches us that calm and a tranquil atmosphere are very favorable for its reproduction. We know that the lower zones of our continent are very humid, hot and have little ventilation and so more favorable for the growth of the *polvillo*. If we gain something in these areas for wheat, we lose it all increasing the strength and number of its enemies. Not more than fifty years ago the fields surrounding Popayán, at an altitude of 22 inches 11 lines of the barometer or 940 toises above sea level, were covered with an excellent quality wheat; but the *polvillo* obliged the residents to elevate their labors, escaping from the desolation of their harvests caused by this plant. What has happened in Popayán, and what caused its laborers to climb to a somewhat higher altitude, is what exiled from Neiva, Patia, Cali, Antioquia, Cartagena, etc. the planting of wheat. It was necessity, then, the sad effects of a microscopic moss and not preoccupation that has established the lower level of cultivation of this precious grain. Let us be more circumspect in our condemnations, let us respect established practices and let us not be taken by the fury of the philosopher to abandon experience.

Despite all of this it is to be desired that in the lower regions, in those in which the humidity is not considerable, where winds prevail through most of the year, in which forests have been pushed back, some tentative experiments be made. I believe that in the plains surrounding Neiva there are gathered favorable circumstances, and that perhaps abundant harvests of good wheat can be found.

If the blight or *polvillo* has established the lower limit of cultivation of wheat, nature has drawn the upper limit: all land whose altitude exceeds 19 inches 9 lines of the barometer or 1,550 toises above sea level produces a wheat whose black and bitter flour is nearly useless. I have drawn a line at this altitude, similar to the first, and I call it the upper limit of the cultivation of wheat. The spacious and elevated plains of Los Pastos, where many towns of the Province of Popayán and the Presidency of Quito are to be found, touch this limit, and the wheat here is among the worst known. The laborers in these places have nearly abandoned its cultivation, replacing it with oats which prospers there more happily. In the mountain range at whose feet lies Popayán one observes that the wheats of Buenavista, Poblazón, Coconuco, Puracé and Hatofrio are better than those of elevated areas; and that rising up one again finds the wheat with a quality of that in the Pastos—black, bitter and unusable as food for man. It is true that this plant grows in more favorable altitudes, but the laborer sees all his hopes frustrated and finds himself obligated to respect this limit prescribed by nature.

The cultivation of wheat, then, is confined in our nations to a zone 438 toises high that begins at 1,112 toises above sea level and finishes at 1,550. In this small zone the winds are frequent, not to say continuous, the humidity is less and the forests are reduced, circumstances that are necessary to find a good wheat; this is the small region that I find favorable in our environment for this plant, the most precious gift of the Old Continent to America. If we want to escape from these limits, if we want to take it from the favored nations which it has preferred, we expose it to many diseases and death, and for ourselves, lacking this principal nutrient, misery.

Wheat will not grow with utility near the equator except at 1,112 toises of altitude; in Spain, at 40° northern latitude, along the coast, and nearly at the same elevation in Chile. Does this limit descend in proportion to a rise in latitude? Would it form a curve whose extrema are at sea level at 35° or 40° latitude, and at 1,112 toises along the line [equator]? Our knowledge is very limited in this; barometric observations with relation to the fruits of the land barely exist; my travels still do not exceed two hundred leagues; I have never passed 4°36′ of latitude; I know only a small part of the great plan; the veil is barely lifted at an angle, leaving in darkness the rest. It may be that by multiplying the travels and observations in our continent, these great vacuums be filled, these immense lagoons, that at the same time humiliate us, scold our ignorance and urge us to work.

In the proportion that we separate ourselves from the upper limit downwards, we find that the wheat improves by degrees until a certain point such that it begins to degrade in quality until the *polvillo* absolutely ruins our harvests in the lower limit. I have noted with admiration that the elevation of the most excellent wheat is nearly in the center of the zone of its cultivation, equally distant from the upper and lower limits; and I have drawn a third line that I call the limit of the best wheat. The wheat of the plains in Santafé, Tunjuela, Cuarchi and Pesillo is good; better is that of Tupigachi, Tabacundo and Cayambe; excellent that of Chapacual and Pasto; a sensible deterioration begins in Otavalo, Buenavista, Poblazón, Coconuco etc. until in the lower limit it disappears because of the blight. It is necessary to note that the law we have just established admits many modifications; that it is influenced by the humidity, the local conditions of the land, the quality of the land, its proportion of currents of air, the abundance or lack of rain and other precipitation, along with other factors that we could add. But whoever travels with barometer in hand, who observes, who notes facts and compares them will agree that there are unalterable general principles, that there is a plan, a constant universal scale in the goodness of flours; and that, if on some occasion the law is altered, this comes from local, partial or transitory causes.

I have given my greatest attention to wheat, although I have not neglected the other fruits which contribute to our subsistence. I have had multiple occasions to observe the entire extension of the zone of wheat cultivation, and to pass its limits in both directions; this has permitted me to speak with greater knowledge of the distribution of this plant than of the rest that follow.

Where wheat begins to prosper with utility for the laborer, the growth of platano (musa) ends.

The specie we know by the name of guineo (musa paradisiaca) is that which rises the most and touches the lower limit of the wheat zone. In the places where guineo grows best one barely finds modest dominicos (musa sapientum). But the zone of this delicious fruit, this limitless resource of man in the tropics, is much more extensive and knows no other lower limit than the waters of the sea; it is found indistinctly spread through 1,112 toises of perpendicular space above the Atlantic and the Pacific; its quality improves in inverse relation with altitude and deteriorates in direct proportion.

If the platano or the guineo is nowhere seen alongside wheat, sugar cane (saccharum officinalem) does pass the lower limit. I have seen in the same terrain these two useful plants, and beneath the same roof the flour mill and the sugar mill or press. In Quitamba and Santiago, near Ibarra sugar cane is cultivated together with wheat. The highest elevation at which I have found this plant, origin of our innocent pleasures as well as our vices, is at 1, 144 toises above sea level; this is its upper limit, and like the platano extends its domicile to the ocean, and improves and deteriorates in the same proportion.

The potato (solanum tuberosum), the most precious gift, according to the expression of Bomare, that America has made to the Old Continent, is grown at the highest altitudes of the globe. In all parts where man has raised his industry, this generous plant has followed. Less delicate than wheat, it has not feared the rigors of the cold nor the eternal ice of the Torrid Zone, and we do not know the limit of its resistance; who knows if as the moss, lichens and other cryptogams it would grow well and with utility at the upper limit of vegetation of our globe beneath the line. If we do not know the limits of the region that the potato loves most, we do know that the lower limit does not pass that of the mildly temperate nations; from 24 barometric inches downward this precious plant is seen no more and is confined in the tropics between 747 toises above sea level and the limit of perpetual snow.

Oats (ordeum distichum), which in the elevated nations plays the role similar to platano in the temperate and hot zones, supporting the necessities of man, as does that plant [platano] below the limits of wheat; but the upper level rises much more, and like the potato follows man to the highest elevations.

Yuca (jatropha mannioc), loyal companion of the platano, follows it everywhere, improves and deteriorates with it and grows within the same limits.

Cacao (teobroma), the patrimony of Guayaquil, Cucuta and Timana, the plant which provides the basis of the most delicious drink, and of which man as yet has not made abuse, is confined to the hot and humid nations of our continent. The greatest elevation at which I have found it is 25 inches of the barometer or 475 toises above sea level; this number expresses the height of the zone in which its cultivation is limited with reference to the coast.

Maize (zea maiz), the most important grain of the new world, and without contradiction more useful than wheat and oats, is also the plant whose growth extends throughout the widest limits. It does not fear the cold as do platano and sugar cane, nor the heat as does the potato; it is found besides wheat and oats in the higher villages as well as besides cacao and yuca in the hot areas; in all places where there are men there is maize. From Riobamba, the highest village that we know, to Cartagena and Guayaquil, in all possible temperatures, in all atmospheric pressures, we are accompanied by this precious plant, this resource for our necessities, this inexhaustable source of delicious and varied compositions. At sea level, where man has not been able to establish wheat, or rather where a powerful enemy does not permit it to grow, maize raises its stalk to six or seven varas [one vara equals approximately 2.8 feet]; in the temperate zone it does not grow as high and its fruit is ready in eight months; in the cold and elevated areas its height is barely one vara and even less, and it is only ready to harvest at twelve or thirteen months. This law is so constant, that maize might well serve to indicate approximately the degree of temperature and altitude of the soil, by way of the length of its growing period and height of its stalk.

This subject is vast; one man alone can not give it the final touch; the aid of many is needed, and many years so that we might flatter ourselves as having a complete distribution of all the fruits that we grow. What can we say of the distribution of all the plants that our soil produces? I am certain that many generations will pass until Botany can signal the limits which confine each vegetable. I present this small essay of the principal fruits which give us sustenance, as an imperfect draft of what must necessarily be perfected. The altitudes I establish as limits of growth of the plants named are not invariable, they are only the result of my observations in the short extension of two thousand leagues. When new observations and new travellers give us more insight, perhaps we will need to change the limits we have mentioned. Meanwhile, I hope that these small efforts are received with kindness and as the fruit of the application of a man who loves the sciences and his country.

Quito. April 6, 1803.

APPENDIX C
BIOGRAPHICAL NOTES

CALDAS HAD NUMEROUS ACQUAINTANCES, friends and colleagues who in one way or another affected the course of his career. In this appendix biographical notes for these persons are presented. Many of these notes are translations of information presented in Arias de Greiff et al. (Ed.), *Cartas de Caldas* (Academia Colombiana de Ciencias Exactas, Físicas y Naturales. Bogotá. 1978), and will be designated by (Cartas) following the note.

AMAR Y BORBON, ANTONIO
Amar y Borbon was Viceroy of Nueva Granada from 1803 to 20 July 1810 when he was overthrown by the revolutionary movement. Expelled from Bogotá, he and his wife returned to Spain. (Cartas)

ARBOLEDA, ANTONIO (B. ?, D. 1825)
Arboleda was a native of Popayán where he began his studies. He finished in Bogotá receiving a degree in law. Arboleda returned to Popayán in 1793. He demonstrated interest in poetry and science, and participated in the revolution. In 1812 he traveled to Antioquia where he was vice-president of the provincial Congress. Following the royalist victory at Cuchilla del Tambo, Arboleda was obliged to surrender his command post in Cali. He was sent to Bogotá and later exiled to Spain, from which he returned in 1825. Arboleda was an intimate friend of Caldas, whom he accompanied on the famous expedition to the Puracé volcano where Caldas's method for measuring altitudes with the thermometer originated. Arboleda represented Caldas in the latter's marriage ceremony. (Cartas)

ARROYO, SANTIAGO PÉREZ DE (B. 1775, D. 1845)
Arroyo was born and died in Popayán. He studied in Popayán and finished law in the Colegio del Rosario where he was vice-rector in 1804. Following independence he was a judge, member of the provincial assembly, acting governor of Popayán and member of the national congress. He made meteorological observations, wrote instructional materials and a history of Popayán during the war of independence. (Cartas)

BARAHONA, MARIA MANUELA (B. 1790, D. ?)
Barahona was born in the hacienda Peredias to the north of Popayán. She was married to Caldas in May 1810. They had four children—Liborio, Ignacia, Juliana and Ana Maria. One daughter—Ignacia—and their only son—Liborio—died in infancy. Ana Maria never married. Juliana married a relative and gave birth to the only direct descendents of her father.

BONPLAND (B. 1773, D. 1858)
Bonpland's real name was Amado Gujeau. A physician by profession, Bonpland took a profound interest in botany. Humboldt covered Bonpland's expenses on

their excursion through Spanish America. Caldas spent a month in the company of Bonpland at the hacienda of the Marques de Selva Alegre near Quito. Bonpland returned to Europe with Humboldt but later traveled to Paraguay where he was taken prisoner for ten years. Following his release, Bonpland took up residence in Uruguay where he lived until his death.

CARONDELET, LUIS FRANCISCO HECTOR, BARON DE (B. ?, D. 1807)
At a young age Carondelet joined the Spanish militia. He participated in the expedition to Algeria and in the capture of Panzacola (today Pensacola, Florida). From 1788 to 1792 he was governor of San Salvador, and later of Louisiana where he confronted the interests of the United States. At the end of 1797 he was named President of the Audience of Quito. Carondelet supervised the reconstruction of the city of Riobamba, the Cathedral of Quito and the construction of a route to the Pacific coast via Malbucho. During his government, Carondelet received Humboldt and Bonpland, and supported Caldas. (Cartas)

CAVANILLES, ANTONIO JOSÉ (B. 1745, D. 1804)
A Spanish botanist and Jesuit priest, Cavanilles was the author of important works in botany. He was Director of the Jardín Botánico of Madrid, and upon his death was succeeded by Francisco Antonio Zea, whom Cavanilles had named as his assistant. During Cavanilles's tenure the herbarium was increased to 12,000 species. He established the genus Caldasia. Cavanilles was a friend and supporter of Mutis. (Cartas)

CORRAL, JUAN DEL (B. ?, D. 1814)
A native of Mompós, del Corral lived in the province of Antioquia when the revolution broke out in 1810. He traveled to Bogotá as a representative and returned to Antioquia in 1812. Owing to the advances of the Spanish commander, Juan Samano, del Corral was named dictator of Antioquia and organized the defense of the province. He employed Caldas as an engineer. When the dictatorship came to an end, the legislature conferred upon del Corral constitutional powers, which he used until his death in 1814. (Cartas)

DOMINGUEZ, BENEDICTO (B. 1783, D. 1868)
Dominguez was born and died in Bogotá. He studied law in San Bartolomé but never exercised the profession. He studied physical science and mathematics in the school directed by Bernardo Anillo. Dominquez colaborated with the *Semanario.* He miraculously saved his life during the reconquest. Beginning in 1813 Dominguez calculated almanacs for Nueva Granada. He was a member of the Academia Nacional de Colombia and was Director of the Astronomical Observatory.

ENRILE, PASCUAL DE (B. 1772, D. 1839)
Born in Cadiz, Enrile served in the Spanish Navy, and in 1809 joined the army during the war of independence against Napoleon. He was chief of staff and second in command to General Pablo Morillo in the expedition to reconquer the Spanish American colonies. As a scientist, Enrile was noted for geodesic measurements performed in Cataluna. (Cartas)

FERNANDO VII — KING OF SPAIN
Son of Carlos IV and Maria Luisa de Parma, Fernando was proclaimed Prince of Asturias in 1789, and assumed the throne following his father's abdication in 1803. Fernando laid his crown at Napoleon's feet in Bayona. Upon his return to Spain in 1814 he established an absolute monarchy. (Cartas)

HUMBOLDT, FRIEDRICH WILHELM HEINRICH ALEXANDER VON (B. 1769, D. 1859)
Born in Berlin, Humboldt was the son of well-to-do Prussian nobility. At an early age he took an interest in a wide variety of subjects—botany, mining, galvanism. He traveled throughout Europe and wrote extensively. In 1799 Humboldt sailed to the Spanish American colonies accompanied by Bonpland. They returned to Europe in 1804. Caldas had direct access to Humboldt from January to June 1802. In Europe Humboldt spent twenty-five years publishing his travel journals. He is recognized as one of the founders of modern geography and brought attention to the study of the Americas. Humboldt presented his broad view of science and nature in the book *Kosmos*.

LOZANO, JORGE TADEO (B. 1771, D. 1816)
Lozano, a native of Bogotá, was a descendent of Spanish nobility. His brother carried the title of Marques de San Jorge. Lozano studied chemistry, mineralogy and botany in Spain. He returned to Bogotá as a physician and substituted for José Celestino Mutis in the chair of mathematics at the Colegio del Rosario. Lozano was a member ad honorem of the Botanical Expedition. His main area of study was zoology and he wrote on the Fauna Cundinamarquesa.

MONTES, TORIBIO
Montes was a Field Marshall who became President and Captain General of Quito upon appointment by the Regency Council of Cadiz. He ordered the execution of Nariño, but his subordinates did not carry this out, so Montes sent Nariño to prison in Spain instead. Montes tried to save Caldas's life by ordering the latter's transfer to Quito where Caldas could live with his brother. (Cartas)

MONTUFAR, CARLOS (B. ?, D. 1816)
Son of the Marques de Selva Alegre. Humboldt was a guest of Montufar's father during his stay in Quito. The Marques asked Humboldt to let young Montufar accompany the European's expedition. Caldas was irritated when Humboldt agreed. Montufar was educated in Spain and returned as a commisioner to maintain the authority and principles of the Junta of Seville against Napoleon. Following the murders of 2 August 1810 in Quito, Montufar formed part of the governing Junta, joining the republican cause. In the struggle against the Spaniards he was taken prisoner and exiled to Spain along with Nariño, but he escaped in Panama, returned and joined the army. Montufar was executed in Popayán on 3 September 1816. (Cartas)

MORILLO, PABLO (B. 1778, D. 1837)
A native of Fuentesecas in the Spanish province of Zamora, Morillo had a brilliant military career from soldier to field marshall and lieutenant general. He was named head of the forces of reconquest and distinguished himself for his bloodthirsty character which provoked the reaction of the creoles in favor of independence. After suffering defeat at the hands of Bolivar, Morillo returned to Spain with the titles of Conde de Cartagena and Marques de La Puerta, and was Captain General of Madrid and Nueva Castilla. Morillo died in France. (Cartas)

MUTIS, JOSÉ CELESTINO (B. 1732, D. 1808)
Mutis was born in Spain. He received a degree in medicine but also studied botany. In 1760 he traveled to America as the personal physician of Viceroy Messia de la Zerda. Mutis began his own botanical investigations which he communicated to the Spanish scientific community and to Linnaeus. In 1783, with the support of Viceroy Caballero y Gongora, Mutis gained the approval of Carlos

III for the establishment of the Botanical Expedition. Mutis worked principally on the medicinal and botanical aspects on cinchona bark, and on his grand opus— the Flora de Bogotá. The Expedition, in Mutis's conception, was a broad scientific institution. As such he promoted interest in the sciences among young Grana-dians. Caldas often referred to Mutis as "my father." The construction of the Astro-nomical Observatory was a personal initiative of Mutis in favor of Caldas. Mutis died without publishing his major works, which finally were published begin-ning in 1952.

MUTIS, SINFOROSO (B. 1773, D. 1822)

A native of Bucaramanga, Sinforoso was a nephew of José Celestino Mutis. In the elder Mutis's scientific testament, Sinforoso was named director of the botan-ical section of the Expedition. He was taken prisoner in 1816 and ordered to arrange the archives and herbaria of the Expedition for their shipment to Spain. He was sent to do forced labor in Cartagena. Sinforoso Mutis died in Bogotá. (Cartas)

NARIÑO, ANTONIO (B. 1765, D. 1823)

A native of Bogotá, Nariño is known as the Precursor of Independence. His trans-lation of the Rights of Man caused him trouble and hardship. Social gatherings were common in his home, with Nariño showing an interest for the sciences. As President of Cundinamarca he maintained hostilities with the Congress of Tunja, sent troops commanded by Baraya and including Caldas. The civil war ended with Nariño's victory, which forced Caldas to flee to Antioquia. Nariño later led a campaign to the South where he was taken prisoner and sent to Spain. Upon his return in 1821 he was named vicepresident and, as such, installed the Con-stitutional Congress of Cúcuta. (Cartas)

POMBO, JOSÉ IGNACIO DE

Pombo was born in Popayán to the Spaniard Esteban Pombo and Beatriz O'Donnel. Thus, Pombo was brother to Lino de Pombo, Caldas's first biographer. He moved to Cartagena where he became a merchant and amassed his fortune. Pombo employed his influence and wealth in the creation of the Consulate Tri-bunal of which he was director, in the promotion of the Dique Canal, in the intro-duction of a printing press for the use of the Consulate (of Cartagena), in the study and commerce of cinchona bark, in improving animal breeds, in the navi-gation of the Atrato River, and in the exploration of a route between the Atlantic and the Pacific. He supported Mutis, the Botanical Expedition and especially Caldas for trips, instruments and investigations. Pombo died in Cartagena. (Cartas)

POMBO, MIGUEL (B. 1779, D. 1816)

Born in Popayán, Pombo studied there and in Bogotá where he received a degree in law and studied natural history. He was an assistant with the Botanical Expe-dition. Pombo formed part of the Supreme Junta that took power on 20 July 1810 and collaborated in the Diario Político of Caldas and Joaquin Camacho. He was lieutenant governor of Bogotá in 1811, prosecutor with the treasury and interior tribunes, member of the congresses (federalist) of 1812 and 1813. Pombo was exe-cuted in Bogotá. (Cartas)

RESTREPO, JOSÉ FELIX DE (B. 1760, D. 1832)

Born in Envigado (Antioquia). Restrepo was Caldas's professor in the Seminario in Popayán. He awakened Caldas's interest in science. Later he was a member of the Antioquian Congress where he proposed the abolishment of slavery. He presided over the constitutional congress of Villa del Rosario de Cucuta and was a member of the Supreme Court. Restrepo died in Bogotá. (Cartas)

Rizo, Salvador (b. ?, d. 1816)

Rizo was the director of the Expedition's painters. He functioned as a sort of chief of staff for Mutis who had great confidence in him, to the point that Rizo received Mutis's scientific testament. Later, Rizo joined the expeditionary force to Venezuela commanded by Simón Bolívar. He was executed on 12 October 1816.

Torres, Camilo (b. 1766, d. 1816)

Torres's was the most powerful mind of the emancipation of Colombia. Born in Popayán, his mother was first cousin of Caldas's mother. He began his studies in Popayán and finished his degree in law in the Colegio del Rosario, where he was vice-rector in 1792. Torres was the author of the well-known Memorial de Agravios (Petition of Grievances). He was member of the Supreme Junta in Bogotá, later President of the Congress of the United Provinces and in that position appreciated the genius of Bolivar. When Bogotá fell, Torres traveled to Cauca [Popayán] and with the other patriots tried to reach shipboard in Buenaventura. Brought to Bogotá, he was shot in the back, his head was severed and displayed in a cage. (Cartas)

Valenzuela, Eloy (b. 1756, d. 1834)

A native of Giron, in the Province of Santander, Valenzuela studied in the Colegio del Rosario where he was later professor of philosophy. He was a member of the Botanical Expedition from its creation until he retired due to ill health in August 1784. Valenzuela was a priest in the city of Bucaramanga (Santander) and one of Mutis's most learned disciples in the natural sciences. Among his works special mention should be given to his *Flora de la Parroquia*.

Zea, Francisco Antonio (b. 1770, d. 1822)

A native of Medellín (Antioquia), Zea studied in Bogotá, and in 1786 was named professor of natural history in the Colegio del San Bartolomé. He was a member of the Botanical Expedition until sent prisoner to Spain as a consequence of the scandal surrounding Narino's publication of the *Declaration of the Rights of Man*. Following two years in prison he was freed and sent to France on a scientific mission. When he returned to Spain he asked permission to travel to America. Instead, Zea was named Professor of Botany and later Director of the Jardín Botánico of Madrid (1804). Zea died in England. (Cartas)

BIBLIOGRAPHY

PRIMARY SOURCES

Arias de Greiff, Jorge et al. (Ed.). *Cartas de Caldas*. Academia Colombiana de Ciencias Exactas, Físicas y Naturales. Bogotá. 1978.

Caldas, Francisco José de. *Semanario Del Nuevo Reino De Granada*. Biblioteca Popular de Cultura Colombiana. Four Volumes. Bogotá. 1942.

Fonnegra, Gabriel (Ed.). *Mutis y La Expedición Botánica* (Documentos). El Ancora Editores. Bogotá. 1983.

Hernández de Alba, Guillermo (Ed.). *Archivo Epistolar Del Sabio Naturalista Don José Celestino Mutis*. Four Volumes. Instituto Colombiano de Cultura Hispánica. Bogotá. 1983.

Obras Completas de Francisco José de Caldas. Universidad Nacional de Colombia. Imprenta Nacional. Bogotá. 1966.

Pérez Arbelaez, Enrique (Ed.). *Alejandro Humboldt en Colombia*. Instituto Colombiano de Cultura. Bogotá. 1982.

Posada, Eduardo (Ed.). *Cartas de Caldas*. Biblioteca de Historia Nacional. Volume 15. Imprenta Nacional. Bogotá. 1917.

————. *Obras de Caldas*. Biblioteca de Historia Nacional. Volume 9. Imprenta Nacional. Bogotá. 1912.

Von Humboldt, Alexander. *Ideas Para Una Geografía De Las Plantas Mas Un Cuadro De La Naturaleza De Los Países Tropicales*. Jardín Botánico 'José Celestino Mutis'. Bogotá. 1985.

SECONDARY SOURCES — BOOKS

Barrig Villalba, A. M. *Algo Sobre el Invento de Caldas*. Arboleda y Valencia. Bogotá. 1915.

Bateman, Alfredo D. *El Observatorio Astronómico de Bogotá*. Universidad Nacional de Colombia. Bogotá. 1953.

————. *Francisco José De Caldas: El Hombre y El Sabio*. Departamento de Caldas. Colombia. 1954.

Etchecopar, Carlos A. and Pérez Montero, Carlos. *El Primer Observatorio de Montevideo*. Montevideo. Instituto Histórico y Geográfico del Uruguay. 1955.

González Pérez, Marcos. *Francisco José De Caldas y La Ilustración en la Nueva Granada*. Ediciones Tercer Mundo. Bogotá. 1984.

González Suarez, Federico. *Un Opúsculo de Caldas: Páginas de Historia Colombiana*. Academia Colombiana de Historia. ABC. Bogotá. 1944.

Gredilla, A. Federico. *Biografía de José Celestino Mutis y sus Observaciones Sobre las Vigilias y Sueños de Algunas Plantas*. Academia Colombiana de Historia. Plaza and Janes. Bogotá. 1982.

Henao, Jesús María and Arrubla, Gerardo. *Historia de Colombia*. Two Volumes. Academia Colombiana de Historia. Plaza and Janes. Bogotá. 1984.

Lafuente, Antonio and Mazuecos, Antonio. *Los caballeros del punto frío: Ciencia, política y aventura en la expedición geodesica hispanofrancesa al virreinato del Peru en el siglo XVIII*. Madrid. Serbal. 1987.

Middleton, W. E. Knowles. *A History of the Thermometer and Its Uses in Meteorology.* The Johns Hopkins Press. Baltimore. 1966.

Paredes, Jaime. *Caldas.* Librería Siglo XX. Bogotá. 1946.

Pérez Arbelaez, Enrique. *José Celestino Mutis y la Real Expedición Botánica del Nuevo Reyno de Granada.* Instituto Colombiano de Cultura Hispánica. Bogotá. 1983.

Schumacher, Hermann A. *Biografía Cultural del Sabio Caldas.* Banco de la Republica. 1969.

――――. *Mutis, Un Forjador de la Cultura.* Traducción de Ernesto Guhl. Empresa Colombiana de Petroleos, ECOPETROL. Bogotá. 1984.

Vezga, Florentino. *La Expedición Botánica.* Carvajal & Cia. Cali. 1971.

Secondary Sources – Articles

Albis, Victor S. and Martinez Chavez, Regino. "Las investigaciones meteorologicas de Caldas." *Quipu.* Volume 4. 1987.

Arias de Greiff, Jorge. "Algo Mas Sobre Caldas y Humboldt." *Boletín de la Sociedad Geográfica de Colombia.* Volume 27. Number 101. 1970.

――――. "El Diario Inédito de Humboldt." *Revista de la Academia Colombiana de Ciencias Exactas, Físicas y Naturales.* Volume 13. Number 51. 1969.

――――. "Una Carta de Caldas a Humboldt." *Boletín de la Sociedad Geográfica de Colombia.* Volume 26. Number 99. 1968.

Bateman, Alfredo D. "Caldas y la Hipsometria." *Suplemento de la Revista de la Academia Colombiana de Ciencias Exactas, Físicas y Naturales.* Librería Voluntad. Bogotá. 1958.

Glick, Thomas. "Science and Independence in Latin America." *Hispanic American Historical Review.* Volume 71. 1992.

Hernández de Alba, Gonzalo. "La Medicina Tradicional en la Expedición Botánica del Nuevo Reino de Granada." *Quipu.* Volume 1. Number 3. 1984.

Humboldt, Federico Alejandro Baron de. "Geografía de las Plantas o Cuadro Físico de la Regiones Ecuatoriales." *Revista de la Academia Colombiana de Ciencias Exactas, Físicas y Naturales.* Volume 8. Number 29. 1950.

Jaramillo Arango, Jorge. "Estudio Critico Acerca de los Hechos Básicos en la Historia de la Quina." *Revista de la Academia Colombiana de Ciencias Exactas, Físicas y Naturales.* Volume 8. Number 30. 1951.

McIntyre, Loren. "Humboldt's Way." *National Geographic.* Volume 168. No. 3. September 1985.

Morillo, Luis María. "El Amor y la Sabiduría de Francisco José de Caldas." *Suplemento de la Revista de la Academia Colombiana de Ciencias Exactas, Físicas y Naturales.* Librería Voluntad. Bogotá. 1958.

Perry Zubieta, Gustavo. "Apuntes para la Historia de las Ciencias Básicas en Colombia." *Revista de la Academia Colombiana de Ciencias Exactas, Físicas y Naturales.* Volume 14. Number 54. 1973.

Pombo, Lino de. "Francisco José de Caldas, Biografía del Sabio." *Suplemento de la Revista de la Academia Colombiana de Ciencias Exactas, Físicas y Naturales.* Librería Voluntad. Bogotá. 1958.

Secondary Sources – Symposia

Estado Actual de la Investigación sobre Caldas. Universidad del Cauca. Popayán. 1986.

Semana Caldas. Universidad del Cauca. Popayán. 1966. IV. Instituto Colombiano de Cultura Hispánica. Bogotá. 1983.

INDEX

153